I first started following Liz on her excellent YouTube Channel several years ago due to her 'down to earth' way of presenting gardening and homesteading knowledge/experienced based content. Liz's book *Grounded* is a first-hand story about self-sufficiency that also collates literally thousands of tips and practical examples of food gardening and self-reliance in such a way that it is a must-have learning tool for beginner through to advanced. Honestly, get the book and get into it!

Founder of the YouTube Channel and Blog Self Sufficient Me, **Mark Valencia** has been a lifestyle, self-sufficiency, and gardening YouTuber/online content creator since 2011

A lovely description of making a new life through restoring health to soil and body, while finding a calm peace – so much about what we need now. Lovely insights into the deeper feelings aroused by gardening, and the rhythm the couple have found.

Charles Dowding, no dig gardener and author of many books, including *No Dig Organic Home and Garden*

Grounded is a refreshingly honest and entertaining read that weaves together personal experience and practical food-gardening tips. It's a modern, yet down-to-earth, guidebook for aspiring smallholders on par with John Seymour's *The Fat of the Land*.

Tanya Anderson is the author of *A Woman's Garden* and the popular gardening and beauty personality behind Lovely Greens

Immerse yourself in this engagingly written story of how Liz Zorab turned her life round and created an almost self-sufficient homestead on less than an acre of land. You'll also learn a lot about gardening along the way. Whether you're already working towards feeding yourself from your garden or haven't yet started growing-your-own, you'll find this book entertaining, informative and inspiring.

Alexandra Campbell runs the Middlesized Garden blog and YouTube channel

"Giving nature a space to be safe." In my opinion, that is the single most important perspective one can have when it comes to gardening. That is precisely why Liz has had the abundance to show for it. Dedication, time, energy and a little money to start with, are all needed to be able to live from your garden. There are several ways to interpret the word 'Grounded', but being connected with the Earth in whichever way that you feel comfortable is the way to go. Liz has captured that in the true essence of its form. If you are asking yourself, "What would it be like to live out my dream of being self-sufficient ?", then get your dirty hands on a copy of Liz´s book and you'll follow her journey from the beginning ... the journey you are on yourself today."

David Trood
AKA The Weedy Gardener

Do you dream of a big garden space with chickens and ducks mixed in? In this book Liz proves that this dream can come true and she doesn't keep the journey and its lessons a secret. A big part of gardening is failing. Yes, it takes seasons of planning, implementing, then missing the mark before you start to really appreciate the garden. Liz takes the readers of *Grounded* from the blank slate of her small homestead in the early years up to now with lots of lessons along the way. I believe every gardener will still need to make some of their own mistakes, but by reading and learning from this beautifully laid out book, perhaps they can make less. The lessons and tips in *Grounded* should help a new gardener get 'good at it' years faster than if they were to do it on their own. From starting small with free or inexpensive garden supplies, all the way up to propagating plants from seeds or cuttings from your own garden. There's even information on how to take your garden goods to market should that be a part of your dream. On a side note, I love books with lots of pretty pictures and this one did not disappoint!

Blake Kirby, Daddykirbs Farm – A Homesteading Story (YouTube)

A very special book that deserves a spot in any gardener's library. Beautifully written, it takes you on a journey on how gardening completely changed one lady's life. If you are looking to learn the principles of permaculture, this book is for you. Liz provides hints, tips, and permaculture principles so that you too can grow nutrient-dense food at home while sustaining the biodiversity within your garden. A MUST read for any serious gardener.

Tony O'Neill, CEO Simplify Gardening.
SimplifyGardening.com

Liz Zorab's guide makes growing your own food and becoming self-sufficient accessible to everyone. Whether you're a city slicker who has never been able to care for a houseplant or a lifetime gardener, this book is jam-packed with information that we all will find useful.

Morgan Gold, Gold Shaw Farm

In *Grounded*, Liz Zorab unfolds the history of her garden's creation. But also, the deeper story of how we change the landscape, and in doing so, change ourselves. Filled with important lessons learned along the way, the reader can be gently educated about permaculture, frugal gardening, and intentional living. But more importantly, they will always be entertained by Liz's joy of growing and relatable worries.

Serina Nell, You Can't Eat the Grass

Richard G. Scott once said that 'to be humble is to be teachable'. Liz Zorab's *Grounded* guides us through five years of a gardener's journey, the highs and the lows, and the immense sense of accomplishment and success in living a humble and simple life on a smallholding in East Wales. On her garden journey, Liz Zorab has managed to conquer one of the hardest feats of any gardener and turn overwhelm into over-abundance in such a short space of time. *Grounded* humbly teaches us to instil the principles of permaculture and simple gardening into our everyday lives.

Adam Jones, Adam yn yr ardd

I paused after nearly every paragraph in *Grounded* due to my mind drifting away, inspired with ideas for growing food on my homestead. The details of Liz Zorab's journey toward food resilience while struggling with health issues eliminates all excuses for the reader and serves as my motivation for making vegetables and fruit a bigger part of my sustainability efforts. *Grounded* is essentially a 200 page enlivening call-to-action: Get out and plant!

Dan Ohmann, The Grass-fed Homestead

If you've ever tried to grow a strawberry or carrot you will be in awe of Liz's achievements. To imagine that a tiny plot could produce enough food to rely on all year is ambitious, but to make it happen, whilst battling debilitating illness, is astonishing. Liz guides us through compost recipes and what to plant where, but her book is as much a guide on how to approach life as it is about permaculture. Rather than lose faith in the face of failure, she uses it to stoke her passion. This book shares a lot about horticulture ... and life.

Simon Biagi, TV presenter

An intriguing hybrid between a storybook and reference manual, Liz has managed to pack in plenty of tips, all weaved into her relatable journey in building a homestead. But don't assume she means homestead on a large scale, there are oodles of take home tips for any space. She offers simple solutions, well explained, and with a warmth that will soon get you growing!

Michael Perry, Mr Plant Geek

What a beautiful book this is; honest, uplifting, practical, and full of inspiring projects, which I cannot wait to try in our own back garden. The author's 'can-do' attitude, her openness, and her willingness to learn and adapt as she goes along, shine throughout. Most of all, I love the way Liz and her husband have gone the extra mile to work with nature. The results, on so many levels, are remarkable.

Brigit Strawbridge Howard,
author of *Dancing with Bees*

GROUNDED

A Gardener's Journey to
Abundance & Self-Sufficiency

Liz Zorab

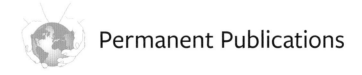
Permanent Publications

Published by
Permanent Publications
Hyden House Ltd
The Sustainability Centre
East Meon
Hampshire
GU32 1HR
United Kingdom
Tel: 01730 776 582
           International: +44 (0)1730 776 582
Email: enquiries@permaculture.co.uk
Web: www.permanentpublications.co.uk

Distributed in North America by
Chelsea Green Publishing Company, PO Box 428, White River Junction, VT 05001, USA
www.chelseagreen.com

Designed by Two Plus George Limited, info@twoplusgeorge.co.uk

Cover photograph by Jason Ingram, www.jasoningram.co.uk
Cover design by Gail Harland

Printed in the UK by Bell & Bain, Thornliebank, Glasgow

All paper from FSC certified mixed sources

The Forest Stewardship Council (FSC) is a non-profit international
organisation established to promote the responsible management
of the world's forests. Products carrying the FSC label are
independently certified to assure consumers that they come
from forests that are managed to meet the social, economic and
ecological needs of present and future generations.

British Library Cataloguing-in-Publication Data
A catalogue record for this book is available from the British Library

ISBN 978 1 85623 302 6

ABOUT THE AUTHOR

Liz Zorab spent more than 20 years working with specialist housing charities and in community development, including setting up the first time bank project in the UK. An award-winning gardener, she gained an RHS Silver Medal for a community-led garden featured on BBC's *Gardeners World Live* in 2002.

A health crisis led Liz to turn to her life-long passion for gardening and growing food as a career. She now runs Byther Farm with her husband, Mr J, using permaculture practices with regenerative and instinctive gardening. On less than 0.8 acre, she grows over 80% of the food and drink they enjoy each year, giving them food security, resilience and increased self-reliance. They also sell vegetables via a community supported agriculture model.

She enjoys spending time with her grandchildren, watching rugby, and creative handicrafts and has a distinct dislike of housework.

Liz regularly writes for *Permaculture Magazine*, teaches gardening and self-sufficiency skills and encourages thousands of people to take up their trowels and live their dreams through a vibrant YouTube Channel, Liz Zorab – Byther Farm.

For Mark, Cecily, Hunter and Magnus

CONTENTS

'I was going to create something that worked for us but gave nature, in all its forms, a space to be safe.'

Byther Farm, summer 2020

FOREWORD
BY HUW RICHARDS

It was a warm, early Autumn day in 2018 when I arrived at Byther Farm for the first time. I remember not being able to find the right house and resorted to phoning Liz for directions, only for her to tell me to turn around and look at the woman waving at the other end of the field. A few moments later, I pulled into the drive of a place that would soon become one of my favourite spots.

Anyone who knows Liz personally would agree that she is a fantastic host, and she was encouraging me to have food and a cup of tea after my long journey, but I wasn't hungry because I was aching for a personal tour of the plot. From what I had seen from her videos and reading her blog posts, Byther Farm is perhaps the best working example of realistic small-scale self-sufficiency within the UK. A real gem, nestled at the end of a lane, surrounded by vast monocultural fields. A splash of paradise.

There is something incredibly special about seeing a place for the first time with your own eyes when previously you've only been able to view it on a screen. It brought a great sense of perspective, and I could see just how well Liz had given multiple purposes to every single element on her micro homestead. One example that stands out in my mind is how Liz mulches her paths with wood chips; they make it gentle on the knees as you walk on them, hide the weed membrane underneath, and then once the chips have broken down into compost, Liz scoops them up and places on the surrounding raised beds.

One of the things I love in *Grounded* is learning how Liz instilled permaculture principles right from the start. The information she shares here is gold dust for anyone wanting to grow their own food, expand their range of crops or reach their personal self-sufficiency goals. One of the techniques I cannot wait to try is called a 'Circle of Love' which uses straw bales, compost materials and chickens to create high-quality compost throughout the year.

I think Liz would agree that this isn't a 'how to' book, but one that sows seeds for you to choose your own journey towards self-sufficiency.

Every journey will be different, but the information shared in *Grounded* serves as an invaluable resource every step of the way.

There is also a big focus on attitude, and how one simple change can lead to huge long-term results. For example, Liz always likes to experiment with new methods of growing crops, rather than falling for the same old ways year in, year out. On page 122 she says, "I want to carry on being amazed by nature and the garden", and this is something that every gardener should also want. It is the single biggest factor in how to get the most from your garden – both in terms of productivity and pleasure – something I have focused on with my approach to gardening this year.

I was struck by how much information is in *Grounded* – it covers every single angle of starting from scratch. There are small 'lesson boxes' throughout the book that provide us with nuggets of information that will potentially save us time and money. The beauty of *Grounded* is it provides the mental toolkit needed to unlock homegrown food abundance from an empty or under-used space.

You will get a real sense of how remarkable Liz's journey has been over the last few years: From being crippled by illness, spending weeks in bed, to growing 85% of her family's food in just three years, and now writing a book that describes the entire process... This is not only an inspirational example of self-sufficiency, but also of self-healing. Her journey is nothing short of a miracle.

Not only has she created an abundant and bountiful space that has transformed her own world, but she has also helped hundreds of thousands of people across this planet to grow more food, overcome personal obstacles, and enjoy life with greater fulfilment and friendship. I am more than happy to say that Liz isn't just a close friend, but also a real hero of mine.

Liz teaches us to learn from what has and hasn't worked, and to understand that very often the most significant difference comes down to being open and flexible. She says things as they are and her transparency makes for a refreshing read, turning negatives into opportunities for growth. She keeps it real, and whilst it is easy to dream big about our own growing goals, it's vital we stay grounded if we are to reach them. After all, there isn't much oxygen on Cloud 9. So if you are looking for a book that covers the inspirational transformation of a blank canvas into a food paradise in a few short years whilst being on a tight budget, then look no further.

Huw Richards
Gardening video creator (YouTuber) and author of *Veg in One Bed* and *Grow Food for Free*

PS – You will need a notepad!

INTRODUCTION

A SAFE HAVEN

It took us the best part of two years to find our new home.

We'd spent so many weekends driving around the countryside in the areas we were considering. Somehow, we managed to choose particularly bad weekends for these recce journeys. There was the weekend of the half marathon run across the Severn bridge (we turned around and went home), and the weekend of a Welsh national cycle race, when we ended up crawling along a potentially very pretty country lane, or it might have been if we hadn't been surrounded by cyclists, all trying their level best to cycle up the incredibly steep hill. We couldn't turn round; we just had to carry on driving, very carefully, among the cyclists, going at their pace, and wondering just how long the hill could be. As it turned out, it was a very long hill! Then there was the weekend of torrential downpours when we couldn't see where we were going as the summer rain smashed down on the windscreen so hard that it sounded like a hail storm.

All that driving around like lost tourists eventually paid off; we narrowed down our search to some very specific areas, even to the point of 'this road, but not that one', which in some ways made our house hunting more difficult and in other ways made it much easier.

We had a list of specific qualities that a house needed, for us to consider looking at it. Top of our list was 'a hall'; a proper hall where we could hang coats and store shoes and where muddy boots could sit without getting tripped over as we went in and out of the door. Also top of our list was 'two toilets', preferably a bathroom and shower room, because we felt that, long term, separate cleansing areas would make for a happier relationship. There were quite a few key elements that sat at the top of the list and all of them were potential deal breakers. The house needed to be cosy without being cramped, a large, light and airy kitchen, but a smaller, more intimate lounge. It needed to be an older house because we don't like the plasterboard construction of newer homes and it needed to be detached with no overlooking neighbours as we had felt so constricted by houses all around us in our rented home.

I also wanted some space in a garden to grow some fruit and veg; I didn't care about having a lawn as I don't like them, but enough room for a large veg patch would be great and a little extra for some fruit would be ideal.

Call us picky if you like; we were! Choosing your last home is a serious task; choosing any home is a serious task, but it was one that we didn't want to get wrong, because we're not moving again until we need to sell the house to pay for care in our old age, should that need ever arise.

One Saturday evening, after the estate agent offices had closed for the remainder of the weekend, I noticed a little semi-detached house that had just come onto the market. Semi-detached: not what I wanted, but on paper, everything else looked right. Sunday dragged on, but also gave me the opportunity to do a bit of research about the area surrounding the house, the village and the history of the building – the internet can be a wonderful thing!

By 8.40am on Monday, I had spoken to the estate agent and booked a viewing for midday. Because we are the type of people who would rather be early and have to wait than be late and keep others waiting, we found ourselves driving around the area surrounding the house we were about to view, killing time for almost half an hour.

We spent quite a while looking around the house and tried very hard not to grin too much. It ticked every single box (except being detached), met every essential criterion, and lots of our desirable ones too. On the way home, I was ready to pick up the phone and put in an offer, my heart absolutely ruling my head and I wasn't alone in my feelings. But we are sensible bunnies; life has made us a touch more cynical than when we were young, and our heads told us that we should have another look before making a decision about the biggest purchase of our lives.

So once at home, we did the sensible thing and made a cup of tea. Following a late lunch and much discussion, I phoned the estate agent and booked a second viewing for first thing the following morning. So, the next day we went back to the little white semi-detached for a second viewing.

In the past, second viewings had invariably led us to see the faults, flaws and the way a house just wouldn't work for how we live our lives, so I was fully prepared to be underwhelmed and disappointed. What I wasn't prepared for was to be enveloped in its charm or to feel so certain that I wanted this house to be our next and last home and that Mr J felt exactly the same way.

Over a cup of tea, we were open and honest with the vendors; we explained our financial situation, discussed potential timescales, and said that we were on our way to the estate agent to put in an offer. We left the property and headed straight to the nearest town to search out the estate agent's office to do just that.

Then we drove home to wait for their response, and we waited and waited. The next five hours felt like the longest for years (probably since the day my daughter made me a grandma – but that's another story). When the telephone finally rang, showing the estate agent's number, I felt sick. We had decided not to mess around with cheeky offers; we had simply made the best offer that we could. Mr J and I had agreed and if our offer wasn't enough, we were going to have to practise the 'it's just not meant to be' and 'there's something better out there waiting for us' strategy of coping with the disappointment.

I answered the phone and held my breath; thank goodness the agent spoke fairly quickly or I could have passed out from a lack of oxygen. A few moments later, I informed Mr J that we had indeed just agreed to purchase a little white semi-detached house complete with a Dutch barn, stables, chicken house and tumble-down piggeries on 0.8 acres of land. Much more than enough for a large veg patch and some fruit bushes.

* * *

When Mr J and I met in 2012, I had told him that I quite liked gardening. It was said in one of those passing comments that meant little and hid the truth quite neatly. What I didn't tell him was that I was passionate about gardening and that being outside among trees and shrubs, food and flowers made my soul sing. Mr J told me that he was into 'stuff that was good for the planet' and during our first few months together I slowly got used to lights being turned off as he walked out of a room (even if I was still sitting in it), his insistence on using public transport whenever it was available and his fastidious recycling habits. Looking back, I can see how much we have influenced each other and fortunately it was, I think, in all the positive ways. I became an avid recycler and more often than not, switch off the lights as I leave the room, while he has become more interested in the contents of the garden.

INSTINCT, EXPERIENCE AND PRACTISING PERMACULTURE

I tend to garden by instinct or perhaps it is just trial and error, but either way I am happy to feel my way through and try things and see how they work. Because every garden I have tended has been 'not quite big enough' for what I wanted to do with it, I have always made every area multi-purpose, layering and stacking functions as much as possible, using the natural flow of water to get the best results I can and a multitude of other actions that, over the last few years, I discovered had a name. When I first started learning about permaculture I sat open-mouthed with book in hand, thinking to myself, 'I do that' or 'oh, that's why x,y or z works'. It seems I had been practising permaculture for 20 or more years without knowing about it. I have since undertaken a Permaculture Design Certificate course and filled in many gaps in my knowledge and practices, but the basic premise of how I work hasn't changed: working with nature, not against it.

I first learnt about gardening from watching my father and from Geoff Hamilton on BBC's *Gardeners' World*. It was during the early 1980s that Geoff introduced organic growing methods to the viewers. Prior to that my gardening experience was one filled with chemicals to combat every conceivable pest. I remember my father spraying the roses with foul smelling liquid to combat greenfly and another one for blackspot. Little blue pellets littered the ground of my childhood garden memories and stinky creosote covered the fences. I completely understand why my father turned to the seemingly quick fix bottles and packets, but once I had started to garden my own space, it didn't take long for me to think that something wasn't quite right about zapping every living thing with one chemical treatment or another. I didn't undergo some sudden metamorphosis into an organic gardener; it was a gradual process of unlearning the practices that I had learnt in the early years and acquiring a new understanding of how fragile the balance of pest and predator can be and how I can support that in the garden.

My urge to garden naturally has grown exponentially; the more I see it works in a positive way the more I want to do, or not do, to produce food and flowers that cause the least negative impact on our environment. All the while I feel I am juggling the want to do the right thing as I see it with my ability to achieve it.

LANGUAGE

Throughout this book I use the terms smallholding and homestead interchangeably; smallholding is the word used in the UK to describe a small farm of less than 50 acres and homestead is used elsewhere, often to describe a house and piece of land where the residents grow food and raise animals predominantly for their own use. I really like the romantic vision that is conjured up in my head when I think of a homestead: a welcoming, homely place with a few chickens running around the yard and a kitchen constantly filled with the aromas of freshly baked bread. I know that the reality isn't quite the same.

YEAR ONE

2016

THIS TOO WILL PASS

Mr J moved approximately 100 raspberry canes, all potted up and waiting for their new home, small trees, including hazel, hawthorn and holly, and lots of herbaceous perennials and herbs. This is the start of our new garden in which I intend to grow as much of our food as possible. Over the course of the next few months, I aim to turn a paddock into a productive vegetable garden with a large area for soft fruit. In a year's time we should have enough fruit and vegetables stored to see us through the winter, well, that's the plan. It was blowing a hooley this morning; the winds were up to about fifty miles an hour and Mr J was being buffeted around as he emptied the plants from the van to the sheltered corner that we had chosen for them to rest for the remainder of the winter.

Excerpt from 21st November 2015

FAITH IN THE FUTURE

It was a bit daunting to be faced with a blank canvas garden space, but more than that, it was incredibly exciting. Almost endless possibilities ran through my mind and the strongest of them all was that I was going to create something that worked for us but gave nature, in all its forms, a space to be safe.

View of the paddock when we moved in

THE BODY CONDITION

During 2015 it became apparent that I really wasn't very well. Something wasn't functioning the way it should and by early summer I presented myself to the doctor weighing around five stones (32kg) heavier than I had been at the start of the previous year. I was prepared to hear that I had a severe case of 'cake', but I thought possibly my thyroid had started to malfunction. Testing soon proved the latter to be the case caused by Hashimoto's thyroiditis, a common but unkind condition that attacks the thyroid gland, not only causing it to function increasingly ineffectively, but bringing with it a host of other symptoms and issues. It transpired that I also had Raynaud's Disease and a weak positive test for Lupus (which my mother had suffered with).

It seems that I had been unwell for so long that I hadn't noticed the gradual decline until some of the most basic functions in my body ceased to work properly. My hearing was impaired, vision was getting very poor, hair was falling out, I found it hard to stay awake, my brain was foggy and confused, I became increasingly weak and most worryingly, I was experiencing muscle spasms and jerks over which I had no control – including spasms around my heart. A couple of trips in an ambulance with blue flashing lights made me all the more determined to stay alive long enough to beat this thing that had turned me from an active person full of enthusiasm for life to an inactive, sad blob. There were countless trips to the doctor's surgery and hospital for tests and more tests to rule out several other conditions.

In July I took to my bed, unable to walk more than a few steps at a time, and waited to see whether the medication would help. Researching online I found which vitamins and minerals might help my conditions and slowly, very slowly started to find which ones did nothing much more than give me alarmingly bright yellow urine and which ones helped to improve my physical wellbeing.

Those few months were wretched; I hurt from head to toe and at one point was covered in a rash that felt like I had red hot ants crawling under my skin. Mr J lovingly plastered me in a zinc cream to soothe the burning and itching and helped me put my bed clothes on over the sticky cream. I lay in a sticky, oozy heap for around a month, and all the while my health continued to decline. A year before I had run a half marathon, slowly, but I'd done it and I had enjoyed energetic and active dance and sports activities. In my self-pitying slump, I wondered how on earth I had changed so much and quietly thought to myself that I was dying.

I didn't want to share this fear with Mr J; he had enough to worry about already. It wasn't until January 2018, as we discussed making a video about living with hypothyroidism from a partner's perspective, that we both revealed our shared, but unspoken fear. Having just dealt with the grief of his mother's death, I can only imagine how difficult it must have been for him to feel that less than a year later, he was losing his partner too.

He tells me that for a while, not only was my hearing and sight impaired and thinking more than a little fuzzy, my speech was often slurred. While I thought I was making complete sense as I talked to him, what came out of my mouth was more like 'hmph, ferumph, umph, fumf'.

The lowest point of that year was the four months I spent lying in bed waiting for my body to just start to function correctly. It was miserable for me, but Mr J was also in pain; not only from the sadness of seeing me so ill, but he physically hurt. The muscle spasms that made my body twitch and jerk were having a direct impact upon him. At night while we slept, my arms and legs continued to dance their merry dance, legs kicking, arms flailing. We may have a king size bed, but that simply isn't wide enough to sleep an arm's length from a woman with twitchy, jerky, spasm-inflicted limbs! Mr J was getting bruised by my uncontrolled movements and on more than one occasion a hefty blow to his lower back booted him out of the bed altogether!

It was also the time during which we found this little house with a paddock and started to buy it. More than once I queried the wisdom of buying a home with so much land, if I wasn't going to be able to help look after it, but there's a determined, almost stubborn streak in me that didn't want to let go of my dream of a little house with a big garden.

When we finally got the keys to the house, I promised myself that I would get up and whatever it took, I was going to do this thing.

BLOG

As with everything nowadays, a task that should have taken about an hour has taken me most of the day. I have come to accept that I am slower in my movements than I would like to be and that I get tired very quickly and need to stop and rest regularly. However, I am determined that this will not stop me from doing the things that need doing or the things that I want to do; it will just take me longer to get them done. What has actually happened as I have slowed down is that I have also learnt to enjoy things more and take more pleasure in the things that I do achieve and also in my family, friends and in my surroundings. This, surely, is a better way to be than to be racing from one thing to the next without noticing all the good things in my life. Whilst I could do without many of the effects of being unwell, this has been an unexpected gift.

Excerpt from 8th December 2015

Webs on roses

My overriding memories of the first few months on the small-holding are filled with frustration and joy. Frustration that I couldn't achieve all in a day that I'd like to and joy that I had the time and mental space to explore all the possibilities that this new growing space gave me.

Gratitude is one of those things that seems to have gone out of fashion. As a child my parents made me practise saying 'thank you' in response to a compliment and I'm so glad that they did. Somewhere along the line, it became the norm to brush off a compliment. 'You did a great piece of work', 'Oh, no, it wasn't much' or 'I was going to do it anyway'. How much nicer for the compliment giver would it be to smile and just say 'thank you'? How much nicer for the recipient to feel the compliment, enjoy it and end the conversation on a positive note? I think a simple heartfelt 'thank you' is a powerful thing.

Likewise, noticing the small things, the subtle changes in the environment, a smile from a friend or a neighbour, the way the grass sways in the wind and a myriad of other things, all are worth taking a moment to appreciate.

Cherry sawfly, not the most welcome of visitors, but part of the ecosystem on our homestead

I don't know when I learnt to notice things. Perhaps it was when we took family walks along country lanes and my father pointed out birds nesting in the hedgerows or minnows (or were they sticklebacks?) in the stream. Perhaps it was on holidays in Spain visiting my grandfather, who had retired there, long before it was fashionable. In the 1960s and early 70s, there always seemed to be tar on the beaches, which was so hard to scrub off, and stinging jellyfish washed up on the sand; it was worth looking carefully at the ground in front of me. As I grew older, life got busier, and the children, (ex-)husband and work became the priority and I suspect I noticed the world around me less. When I was forced to slow down, I once again started noticing the world around me in a deeper, more connected way.

Intentional observation can be learnt: spending a few moments sitting, quietly and still, and looking and listening to what is around us. Sometimes I just sit and try to keep my thoughts in the moment; at other times I become so engrossed in the colours, sounds and smells that I feel like I am a part of my surroundings. For a gardener, it is a really useful tool.

My favourite hidden corner (summer 2020)

The paddock was almost empty except for these old trees

The fallen elderberry continues to thrive

MAKING OBSERVATIONS

From our visits to the smallholding while the solicitors did their work during the purchase process, I already knew the arc of the sun in the sky during summer and I quickly learnt exactly where the sun rose and set during the winter months. The land is almost level with a gentle slope of just five feet (1.5m) from one side of the paddock to the other across which the water flows on its way to the River Severn. The wind however is not gentle. There is an almost constant westerly breeze and for a few short weeks each year the wind comes from the east. The fencing around the perimeter was simple stock fencing, providing fantastic views across the fields to the river, but no windbreak and no shelter from the cross winds.

When we moved in there were a handful of trees in the paddock. On the western boundary there is a row of gnarly old plum and damson trees, leaning from the impact of years of air relentlessly pushing against them.

There is also the largest elderberry tree I've ever seen. It too has done battle with the wind and, at some point, it fell over, but enough of the roots remained in the ground to keep it alive. So now the trunk lies on the ground and branches grow vertically from it offering us an impressive display of elderflower blossoms each year.

Apart from the shade provided by these fruit trees, the whole paddock enjoys the sun from dawn until dusk.

On the other side of the smallholding to the paddock is a smaller area, which is home to several very tall sycamore trees and the previous owners had planted a hornbeam hedge around this section.

During the time I was lying in bed waiting for the medicines, vitamins and minerals to work, I spent a great deal of time daydreaming of what I might do with the paddock. I didn't have the dimensions of the potential growing space, so I just had to use my imagination. When I felt strong enough to sit up in bed, I made notes and drew rough sketches and not long before we moved here, I sat on the living room floor surrounded by sheets of flipchart paper and I designed the new garden in its entirety.

Getting to know your site before you start creating your garden allows you to factor into your plan any windbreaks, watering, shade requirements and issues.

FIRST STEPS

The soil we inherited on the site was close to lifeless. I dug out nine small holes, about the size of a spade, in different spots across the paddock and in those nine spadefuls, I found just three worms. This was not what I wanted to see. It was not the sign of a healthy, life-filled environment; it was not teeming with fungal life and small creatures doing their thing. I now knew that my priority was to encourage some life back into the soil.

The very best way that I know to improve the quality of soil is the addition of organic matter, in particular compost with its billions of microbes, fungi and tiny creatures all doing their part to break down the materials and incorporate them into the soil. There was a lot of soil that would need improving, so making compost was a priority.

View of Byther Farm from across neighbouring fields

I found some old pallets in the yard and slowly dragged them into the paddock: a couple of steps forward with the walking stick, turn around, move the pallet and repeat. Having tied them together with string, I started to fill them with anything I could find that would decompose including leaves from the huge sycamores, feathers from old pillows, pony manure that I found in piles and wood shavings that had been bedding for the former owner's animals. I had asked them not to muck out the stable area as I knew that the bedding would make ideal compost.

I recall feeling very strange about starting this process. I had asked Mr J for permission to build a compost heap and he looked at me incredulously and asked why I thought I needed permission. As odd as it may sound, it felt rather surreal to stand in the almost empty paddock and try to envisage what was to come. I couldn't quite believe that this place was ours and that I had the go-ahead to create the garden of my dreams.

One compost bin quickly became two and I also piled the contents of the stable floor in a heap to allow it to rot down.

Pallets were about to become my new best friend and we spent many evenings collecting them from local residents who advertised that they were disposing of them through Freecycle and Facebook Marketplace. Eventually we found a local company who had a stash of pallets that we could have for a donation to their Christmas party fund of just £1 per pallet – no matter what size pallet it was. They were also happy to deliver the pallets, so we soon had a regular supply of heat-treated pallets. Over time they also offered us pallets of approximately 7 feet (2.1m) long and 3 feet (1m) high and some 15 feet (4.5m) long.

The first compost bin, made from recycled pallets

As I wanted to fill the raised beds that were to grow our food in the coming years, I looked at different ways to make compost as quickly as possible. I experimented with different combinations of materials and also tried making three-week compost.

MAKING COMPOST

Nature has a perfect way to return materials to the ground to become food for the future generations of plants. We can mimic this process by making compost.

Compost is made by bacterial action on organic materials for which all that is needed is the materials, water and oxygen; nature will do the rest for us.

A combination of green materials and brown materials will make the best compost in the shortest time.

Layer the materials or mix them together, ensuring that the whole heap is moist, but not constantly saturated with water, and give it some time.

Covering the top of the heap with a tarp, old carpet, cardboard or a deep layer of straw will help ensure that the heap doesn't become waterlogged and keep in the heat that is generated in the composting process.

GREEN MATERIALS

Annual weeds (best when not in
    flower or with seed heads)
Manure
Coffee grounds
Kitchen scraps and peelings (don't
    include any meat products which
    might attract vermin)
Discarded plants from the garden
Grass clippings
Feathers

BROWN MATERIALS

Cardboard
Shredded paper
Egg cartons
Newspaper
Dried leaves
Straw
Wood chips
Sawdust

There are two basic types of composting, hot and cold.

Cold composting is a slower process and can take 12-24 months. It is the more simple method of piling the materials together, watering the heap and leaving it to break down slowly. This method may not destroy any seeds in the compost, so potentially you could be spreading weed seeds back onto your garden if you have thrown weeds in flower or in seed into the heap.

Hot composting is potentially more labour intensive, but it is faster and it raises the temperature inside the heap sufficiently to destroy most weed seeds. Turning the heap will speed up the process by allowing more oxygen into the heap. This is a straightforward process of moving the materials at the top of the heap to the bottom and the outer edges to the centre. Using a pitchfork or garden fork move the layers into a new space or if there is not enough room to do that, use the fork, to move the contents of the heap, mixing it and allowing oxygen to access the centre of the heap.

BLOG

Well, today brought a nice surprise! Flashback to 18th April when Mr J cut the grass in the paddock and I created a new compost heap in a metal hoop made from stock fencing wire.

We layered grass clippings with brown material to the depth of about two and half to three feet. I had intended to turn the heap a few times to add air to it to encourage swift decomposition, but we didn't get a chance to do it because we were busy elsewhere on the smallholding. Mr J and I have watered the compost heap regularly with the water from the ducks' pond and water buckets, so it has had some attention, just not as much as I would have liked.

This afternoon, after the heavy rain had stopped, I thought that if I didn't do something with it, it would stop composting and turn to stinky sludge, which I really don't want to use in our new vegetable beds. We have managed to acquire a couple more pallets (by asking nicely at the local farmer's store and builder's merchants), so they became the sides of the new compost heap. We are already using the compost from our first two heaps in our raised beds, so it is the ideal time to move the location of the compost heaps to the other side of the paddock to be nearer the raised beds.

So, with three pallets strapped together to form a U shape, Mr J and I lifted the wire hoop from around the compost heap that we made on 18th April.

The plan was to put the driest and least composted material in the base of the new heap and the remainder of the partially decomposed heap on the top of it and then water and cover it to allow it to continue to decompose and hopefully in another month or two, it would be ready to use in the garden. But things didn't go quite according to plan because once I cut into the heap with the spade and removed the outer edges and top layer, I found that the centre of the compost heap was, well, compost!

A bit stunned (and delighted) by what we were seeing I dug through it a little and although we can still see a layer of soil and coffee grinds, it is for all intent and purposes ready to use!

So that's it, rich, dark, sweet smelling compost in just 23 days!

Excerpt from 10th May 2016

Starting compost in a hoop of stock fencing

Layers of green and brown materials

Three-week compost

HEDGES AND EDGES

The other priority was to soften the impact of the wind as quickly as I could. To that end I fixed windbreak fabric to the fences wherever I could, to slow down the wind as it moved across the site and to protect the young plants that I planned to get into the ground during the first year. That bright green netting was ugly and I'm glad that it has faded a little over time and is now mostly hidden by foliage for much of the year.

With the help of Jane, one of my most long-standing friends, a hedge was planted around the east and south perimeter during the early spring of our first year. I waited another year before I planted the hedging on the west side. In hindsight I should have planted the west hedge first, but the wind was blowing from the east for those few weeks before planting so it made me inclined to start on that side instead.

It would have been easy to plant a thick, fast-growing evergreen hedge of something like *Cupressus × leylandii*, which would have provided wind shelter quickly, that could be clipped into a neat straight line, but it would also have been a lost opportunity.

Instead I chose varieties that would offer nesting places for birds, flowers for pollinators and bees, and fruits and nuts for us and for the wildlife; after all, a few hundred feet of planting could potentially provide us with a lot of food for years to come. I ordered one-year-old trees from The Woodland Trust, who offered 'tree packs' for those wishing to create new hedges or shelter belts.

Planting those foot-high whips felt like an act of faith in this land. A signal that I believed that we could create something special for us and for the wildlife here.

The initial planting comprised hawthorn, blackthorn, Guelder rose, wild rose, dog rose, hazel, purple willow, wild damson, holly and rowan. I also included some Lombardy poplar because I wanted some instant height and maturity; because of the speed at which they grow they will need to be pollarded (the process of cutting back a tree to a single point on the trunk, at some point well above ground level, which encourages the plant to send out lots of new growth) or removed in the coming years. Each year I have added a few extra fruit trees, like apple, pear and elderflower, to the hedge together with some buddleia to support the dwindling butterfly population.

The potential food forest and flower border in front of the fence, the shrubbery behind it

Planting the hedge on the east and south boundaries

Hedgerow rosehips

Elderflowers fill the air with their sweet fragrance each spring

> The quick fix option
> is not always the best;
> the slower and more
> considered answers
> often give better results.

This colourful medley of trees and shrubs has created a scruffy, tangled hedge, which is ideal for insects to hide in and birds to build nests between the thorny branches. By the end of year two I had started harvesting rosehips from the hedge and by the start of the fifth year, the hedge on the east boundary was five to six feet (150-180cm) high.

PROPAGATING HEDGING PLANTS

Many of the hedging plants are easy to propagate or you can transplant self-sown (volunteer) seedlings into pots to grow on to add to the hedges. Each year I end up with a dozen or more pots with young plants growing in them, biding their time to be large enough to join the tangled mess around the edges.

Hawthorn grows readily from seed; we find the seedlings popping up across the gardens and I move them into pots for a year before adding them to the hedges.

The roses will grow from seeds, but I find it easier to take semi-ripe cuttings in late summer and early autumn.

Young wild damsons have been dug up from where they grow across the garden; presumably their seeds are redistributed by birds.

Willow roots very easily from cuttings pushed into the ground wherever I want them to grow.

Elderflower has been grown from seed; I have tried cuttings without success to date, but I have managed to remove some suckers from the largest tree to transplant into the hedge.

That hedge separates our small plot from the fields that surround us. Maintained by a local farmer, these fields are planted with feed crops some years, and other years they have sheep grazing in them. I have lost hours watching the sheep and their little lambs grazing; they are like a living screensaver moving back and forth across the landscape.

LIVESTOCK AND THEIR POTENTIAL

It hadn't occurred to me how useful some small livestock can be on the smallholding for improving the soil condition and for reducing pests. Watching videos on YouTube gave me plenty of ideas of how I might get the chickens to earn their board and lodgings and I put them to work on the composting materials.

Chickens seem to have the ability to miss the obvious that's right in front of them, but can spot the tiniest of 'somethings' in a pile of poop and straw. That very ability makes them superb mixers, aerators, scratchers and spreaders of materials that can be composted. They will merrily spend hours turning over the ground, leaves or the compost creating a finer and finer mixture as they do.

Once the chickens had dealt with the pile of bedding from the stable, spreading it out over an area at least four times the size of the original pile, I excluded them from that area with a temporary fence made from chicken wire supported by bamboo canes.

Their droppings combined with the straw, hay and wood shavings from the stable made a suitably rich area in which to grow our first potatoes on the smallholding.

I planted the seed potatoes just under the soil and then heaped some of the composted bedding over each one. The thistles started to grow, so I weeded the area and covered the soil with straw. The chickens were often spotted standing outside of the chicken wire fencing staring in at the growing potatoes with their straw duvet. I wondered whether they could see those miniscule edible bits and pieces that they couldn't reach.

In the UK, you cannot feed livestock anything that has been in the kitchen (this also applies to chickens and ducks kept as pets[*]), so no kitchen scraps or peelings were put onto these heaps. Kitchen scraps go into a bin for recycling by the local council, who use it to create biogas to fuel local resources.

Because the chickens found it awkward to get into the compost bins and fully turn over the decomposing materials, we created what we named a 'Circle of Love'.

Putting several bales of straw in a circle in their field, I proceeded to fill it with the used bedding from their houses, leaves, weeds, grass

---

* APHA, www.gov.uk/government/news/apha-warns-not-to-feed-kitchen-scraps-to-farm-animals-because-of-disease-risk

Potatoes growing in ground prepared by the chickens

The Circle of Love

clippings and anything else green and leafy from the garden – all the things that the chickens love. The chickens, now sheltered from the wind from every angle, would then happily spend time in it, scratching about, moving it around and turning it over and over again, making compost speedily.

Every time I mucked out the chicken house, had leafy greens from the garden or fallen apples, they got thrown into the compost inside the straw bales and the chickens would race over to me to see what new delights were on offer to them.

We emptied the Circle of Love of compost several times in the first couple of years, giving us good quantities of organic material to add to the raised beds. When eventually the rain, wind and constant scratching by the chickens broke down the straw bales, we let the chickens incorporate the straw into the contents of the circles of love too.

We had agreed that as smallholders we would not give names to the poultry, that names would be restricted to our pets. Enter our first two, strictly livestock, Aylesbury ducks – Frederick and Mrs Warne.

I secretly named them as we drove home from buying them and it was about two weeks before Mr J caught me chatting away to Mrs Warne about nothing in particular. It didn't take very long before he called them by the names too.

They are Aylesbury ducks, the type that Beatrix Potter wrote about in her delightful children's books. I grew up on a diet of Jemima, Peter, Flopsy Bunnies and Pigling Bland and I just couldn't help myself from naming these enchanting ducks something relating to Beatrix Potter. Somewhere in the back of my mind I recalled that the author had married her publisher. I remembered incorrectly. Apparently she had been engaged to Norman Warne, the third son of Frederick Warne, but he had died before they were married. No matter that I had my facts incorrect, Frederick Warne was the publisher's name on the books and the ducks remained Frederick and Mrs. Warne as a nod to one of my childhood's favourite authors.

We quickly learnt how efficient ducks are at clearing areas of slugs and snails and what a delight they are to have around. Mrs Warne had a penchant for young onions, so it wasn't long before I had started to construct some fencing around the vegetable garden. The flexible poultry netting that we'd found on site had limited success as a barrier because Mrs Warne soon found that if she leant against it, she was able to reach the young green shoots that she so liked, so I turned to pallets once again for a solution.

PLANNING FOR A WHOLE GARDEN, EVERYTHING IS MULTIFUNCTIONAL

From the start we decided to make the infrastructure flexible, move-able and non-permanent. Fences, animal enclosures, raised beds and everything else is potentially temporary to allow us to move, alter and adjust them as our needs change and as we learn more about the land, the livestock and our needs.

During the first year or two I found it frustrating that everything looked so haphazard and temporary, but when it came to making changes, I was relieved that Mr J had insisted on it. Five years into our life here and I'm still making changes to the layout to temporarily accommodate additional numbers of ducks for a short period or to allow for extra growing space for a season. And should, for any reason, we want to return the paddock to just grass, trees and shrubs, we could do that without too many problems.

The vegetable garden was originally going to be a square, but I decided to create it half at a time. We measured out the entire square using all the lengths of string that we could find, then divided it into two. The first half is all that ever got completed as the plans changed and evolved over time and with experience. The process of trial, evaluate, change, monitor, evaluate, has become key to how I run the productive areas on our land. Rather than seeing something as a failure because it hasn't worked as well as I'd like it to, I try to reframe it in my mind as one step in an elimination process to help me find the best way to do something. Perhaps I am fooling only myself, but it enables me to keep on keeping on and not stare into the abyss of failure and beat myself up emotionally about it.

In the vegetable garden there were to be 20 raised beds with wide pathways between them. The raised beds are 4 feet (1.2m) wide with a pathway of almost 3 feet (1m) between them and around them in all directions. I wanted to plan for the future and, at the time that I was drawing up the garden plan, we were unsure whether my health would improve or continue to deteriorate, in which case I might end up in a wheelchair. I still wanted to be able to grow our vegetables and fruit, so pathways that would accommodate a wheelchair seemed to make sense. It is much easier to plan for such eventualities and not need them than to need to redesign and remake the garden at a later date. If I was planning the area from scratch again, I might make those paths even wider because the wildflowers and self-sown herbs and vegetables can sometimes make walking along the paths a little like an

Making the first raised beds

obstacle course. Without a doubt I could remove them all to make the paths clear of invaders, but I think the garden would be poorer for it.

Watching Mr J put those first few raised beds together was incredibly exciting. The vision held in my head was just beginning to take shape. When I looked at the space that was to be the vegetable garden, I could see it filled with food waiting to be harvested; until I blinked and looked properly at the grassy patch of land in front of me. Daydreaming as a means of escape is not, I think, a productive use of time, but daydreaming as a way to turn concepts into more concrete (or in this case wooden) plans is a useful tool.

I struggled intellectually with using plastics in the garden, but in the end decided that I would use weed suppressing membrane on the pathways to reduce the workload at a time when I was having so much difficulty moving around. I also used it in other areas to kill off the weeds with the intention of lifting it again after a couple of years. At the

Creating pathways between the raised beds

Keeping a simple garden journal

time of writing it's been over four years and it's still there, but I do plan to remove it eventually. I don't intend to further justify its use; sometimes we have to do imperfect things to allow us to do other, more important, things. My goal for the first year was to create the garden and start to put food on our table. During the first year we created 10 raised beds.

RECORD KEEPING

I like lists; I like the clarity that they can bring and I use them to help gain a sense of achievement at times when I feel overwhelmed by the amount of work there is to do. There's nothing quite like crossing an item off a 'to do' list, even if I'm also adding five more jobs at the bottom of the page. I try to keep good records, of what I'm growing and when and how, of plans for the future of the garden, the buildings, the livestock. They are priceless when I want to know when x, y or z happened or whether a particular task has been completed.

I keep a garden journal; it's not a romantic as it sounds. I simply list when I have sown seeds, when they germinate, get transplanted and/or harvested. As one growing year blends into the next in my mind, I find the journal the most convenient way to refer back to previous years and compare how the current season fares against previous growing seasons.

I also take photographs and lots of them. As a tool for recalling where I planted plants or seeds, these visual guides are the most accurate that I have. And most recently, I film the garden, allowing me to make notes to myself about my thoughts, hopes and dreams for the garden.

These records allow me to evaluate and where necessary, make changes, to the layout and substance of the garden. That all sounds jolly organised and slightly clinical, but I'm not as organised as I'd like to be with record keeping and for the most part, I use my garden journal, photographs and videos to bolster myself up during the times that I feel like I'm not achieving much or that a particular area of the garden isn't developing as much as I had hoped. There's nothing quite like notes and photos to show you exactly how much has changed in a given period.

> Keep records in a way that makes sense to you. They are good for helping you plan for future years' planting and to remind you how much you've achieved.

NO DIG GARDENING

During the first few months here, my friend Jane and I lifted the turf from a section of the paddock as I wanted to create a perennial herbaceous flower garden running the full width of the shrubbery, but on the other side of the fence. To give Jane the due credit, she did most of the cutting and lifting and removing as I wobbled about with a walking stick and struggled staying upright and awake. I had wanted to fill it with colourful perennial flowers that would reflect the shrubs on the other side.

I wanted a white version of sweet rocket, with its pure white flowers that stand out so boldly in the fading light of the day, to fill the air with their heady scent. Peonies would flounce their way through May and announce the arrival of the perfumed June roses. Delphinium and hollyhocks would add stature and colour at head height, irises and crocosmia would be companions to *Alchemilla mollis* (lady's mantle) while perennial geraniums, geums and nepeta would offer ground cover and a base from which all the other plants could erupt. Despite being given quite a few herbaceous plants and raising several from seeds, the border was not the colour filled thing of beauty that I had imagined. I had hoped for a traditional cottage garden look of plants jumbled in together all jostling and vying for our attention. By the end of the first summer it was filled with weeds that had germinated in the bare soil that had been exposed when we lifted the turf. For a field that appeared to be just grass, it produced an impressive selection of wildflowers and pernicious weeds.

By autumn 2016 I had accepted that this area was not a priority for me (if it had been, I would have tended it more lovingly to stop the weeds when they were small) and that I needed to continue to concentrate on creating the vegetable garden. By early summer 2017, the weeds had outgrown the herbaceous perennials both in stature and in vigour and I resolved to develop the rest of the paddock using 'no dig' methods and leave those weed seeds well and truly buried in the ground.

The paddock, which before we moved here was home to four alpacas and a pony, was by no means just grass. Over the first year I found dandelions, daisies, clover, creeping buttercup and silver buttercup, thistles, tansy and bird's foot trefoil. In the shade of the old wild damson and plum trees there was lesser celandine and stinging nettles, so many stinging nettles.

FINDING LOW-COST RESOURCES

Our budget for creating the growing spaces didn't exist. Not that we had absolutely no money, but I hadn't worked out how much I thought it would cost. What I did know was that I needed to make savings at every step of the way because I was going to have no income until I was growing food and Mr J had yet to find employment. Our meagre savings were all we had and we needed to make them last until there was a household income.

I scoured the internet for salvage yards and items being given away or at a very low price. I spotted an advert for used lengths of timber and without seeing it, I bought a job lot. I had been told that the lengths of wood had a few screws and nails in them and in my optimistic naivety, I imagined that Mr J would be able to remove them in an afternoon or two of work. The reality was that each length had a couple of dozen bent and rusty nails and screws to be removed and getting them ready for use in the garden was a slow and painful process. The last 20 or so lengths of this wood were eventually cut up and used in the woodburner, so it wasn't wasted and the ashes were returned to the ground to improve the soil.

We also found pallets being thrown away and other lengths of wood, a couple of water butts and patio slabs and a host of other useful bits and pieces. It wasn't long before people were offering us all kinds of 'stuff' that they no longer needed. And because I felt awkward about saying no to their kindness, we then had piles of junk here and it became our responsibility to recycle or dispose of it. It has taken me a long time to learn to say 'no thank you', but it's a valuable tool.

There's a fine line between having useful resources to hand and a junk pile. The hoarder in me still finds it hard to recycle items that my gut instinct tells me might be useful – eventually! On the other hand, I have also discovered that I find it stressful to have piles of stuff just lying around and I start to feel weighed down by the imagined enormity of the task ahead to clear away the piles of rejected items. A bit like doing the washing up; it never takes as long as imagined to get cleared away and the hardest part is actually making the decision to do it.

> Local resources can be a blessing, but knowing when to say no thank you is essential.

Recycled wood waiting to have nails and screws removed

THE BIG PICTURE IN SMALL STEPS

In late December 2015 I had stood in the paddock explaining to friends about what the garden would look like. Propped up by walking sticks, I waved my arms around to demonstrate that 'this area will be ...' and 'over there I'll put the ...'; at that point I was crystal clear in my mind about exactly how everything would be and how it would look, but very little of it came to fruition in the way that I had imagined. It is better, much better.

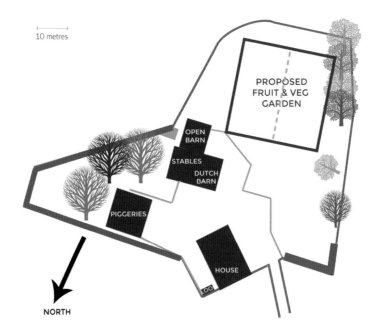

Plan of the property with proposed veg garden

Mr J created the first couple of bed frames from the recycled wood lengths by screwing them together at the ends and where we needed to join two lengths of wood together, he used a joining strip of wood with screws fixed to each of the lengths of wood to create an even longer side to the raised beds. I sourced organic materials to put in them. The compost in the heaps wasn't ready to be used, but my sister offered us as much well-rotted horse manure as we wanted. We just had to collect it. I think we filled the car with bags of beautiful rich black manure compost just twice before we realised that it would take a month of Sundays to fill the beds this way, so I ordered a ton of topsoil.

> Complete one small area at a time so that it is manageable, then move on to the next area.
>
> Keep your back to the area that is still to be cultivated, and face what has been achieved so far. This way you won't get daunted by the size of the task ahead.

One ton of topsoil doesn't go very far in a raised bed measuring 14 feet (4.25m) by 4 feet (1.2m), but between some of the partially decomposed compost, the horse manure compost and the topsoil, I managed to fill the first two raised beds. A further order of topsoil helped to start the next pair of beds.

I put cardboard and paper feed sacks onto the grass before piling the soil and other materials into the beds. Perhaps piling is an exaggeration; 'just about covering the cardboard' would be a more accurate description.

As soon as one raised bed was ready, I planted it with seeds and seedlings. Having something growing in the beds gave me encouragement to continue with the next one. Although I had the overall vision in my head, taking small steps and celebrating each success made the mammoth task ahead seem all the more achievable. I was learning to manage my expectations.

I may have started managing my expectations, but still had a long way to go to manage my imagination of how long any one task might take.

Mr J can be seen to raise an eyebrow when I say 'can we just ...?' or 'it'll only take half an hour'. In my mind's eye the jobs are almost completed by the time I have asked for his help; it's funny how the reality never quite seems to match up to the speed of completion in my imagination.

This might be the moment to mention that I am a truly awful person to do DIY or building work with. I have an idea of what I want to make and how I think it should be done, but almost never manage to convey that concept accurately or even adequately enough for it to be translated into a 3-D functioning object. I resort to talking about a 'thingamebob' or 'oojamaflip' and hand signals and none of those are terribly helpful when trying to create a technically sound piece of work. There is the potential, of course, that this applies not only to DIY or building projects, but to every activity of our lives. I don't intend to ask Mr J about this; I may not like the response!

Early spring 2016: a plum tree we thought was dead

THE JOY OF WOOD CHIPS

I wanted to use wood chips or bark on the paths, but the price of buying them in bags at the local garden centre was prohibitive. We bought a few bags of bark chippings from the local farmers' merchant and having seen how small an area one bag covered, I realised I would have needed many hundreds of bags of wood chips to cover the space I wanted. Finding a local tree surgeon who might drop wood chips to our homestead became a priority (one of very many priorities). We asked for quotes from three local tree surgeons to remove some of the very tall, spindly sycamore trees in the area at the side of the piggeries. One tree was so close to the buildings that it pushed against the guttering, making it squeak and squeal as though it was in pain each time the tree moved in the wind.

The first tree surgeons who visited weren't terribly interested in the job and the second didn't turn up for their appointment with us. The third tree surgeon arrived, gave us a quote, talked to us about the potential for wood chips and it wasn't long before they were hard at work removing the five very tall, troublesome trees from the area by the piggeries.

Tim and Tom, the tree surgeons, agreed to give us wood chips whenever they were working in our area and before long the first load of chipped wood had arrived. I used it on muddy pathways to reduce the chances of slipping and injuring ourselves. It wasn't long before the second, third and fourth trailer loads of wood chips were delivered. They were very good at putting the piles of chips in slightly different places and informing me what kind of wood it was. It turns out that not all wood chips are equal.

> Tea, kindness and chocolate biscuits go a long way to building good relationships.

Anything like leylandii hedging was destined for pathways, the ever-green oak went into the chicken run, and apple and cherry were used in the vegetable garden and in compost heaps.

My plan was that all the wood chips used on the paths in the vegetable garden would be left in situ for at least two years and then, once it had broken down into a fine composted condition, I would scoop it up and add it to the raised beds to increase the organic matter in the soil.

I also added them to the food forest floor to help reduce the weeds and define the areas that were pedestrian and those that had plants. Leylandii wood chip are acidic, so I didn't want to add them to the compost heap in any great quantities; leaving them on pathways to mellow and break down seemed a better option and provided us with something soft underfoot in the meantime.

There are times of the year, in particular in late summer and autumn, when there is a higher percentage of green materials for the compost bins; the growing piles of wood chips gave me ample brown materials to mix with them to create lots of compost.

When Mr J found part-time employment locally, work on building the raised beds slowed and then came to a grinding halt and I needed to find other ways to create beds to plant into. In hindsight I'm not sure why I didn't just put cardboard on the grass and put compost on top of it, but I had it in my head that I wanted the beds to be raised and that is what I focussed on doing.

Without Mr J to help here for much of the day to move heavier objects around, we looked at other ways that I could move everything that I wanted to. I spotted a garden trolley or cart that had a tipping bucket and one handle to pull it along. This would mean that I could still use a walking stick when I needed to, but I would be able to get on with all the jobs that I wanted to tackle while he was at work. We often refer to it as the truck. The truck's arrival was a significant moment, it gave me a new-found freedom and I spent day after day playing with my new toy by moving wood chips and the occasional grandson. Two or three truck-loads of wood chips were about as much as I could manage each day, but that didn't matter: we had found a way to give me some more independence. Not only was it good for my physical health, it was the confidence boost that I needed to keep going throughout the autumn.

We had been visiting the local garden centre most Sunday mornings to collect the largest of the cardboard boxes that they had for customers to take away. They were happy for us to take the larger boxes as they were not of much use to most of the customers. One particular morning we arrived just as a member of staff was putting 30 or more boxes in the recycling area. They were the boxes in which vegetable and bedding plants had been delivered

Cardboard boxes recycled from the local garden centre

to the garden centre. They all had lids and folded flat so we could fit all of them into the boot of our little van and I knew just what I wanted to do with them.

I created some instant raised beds from the cardboard boxes and tried mixing wood chips with topsoil to fill them. I planted seed potatoes and to some extent this was a success. Certainly, we had some potatoes from the boxes, but the plants always looked a bit anaemic and seemed to struggle. I later learnt that it would have been better to plant the potatoes in a small amount of topsoil and cover them with wood chips, rather than mix it in. This is because the decaying wood depletes the soil of nitrogen, but only adjacent to the wood. If the layer is above the soil then only the 1-2ins (20-50mm) area immediately below the wood chips is likely to be affected. When I mixed the chips in, the depletion potentially happened in many small areas throughout the soil making it more difficult for the potato plant roots to feed well. Lesson learnt, the next year I used the wood chips as a mulch.

I made another bed in boxes for runner beans; the boxes smothered the weeds and, filled with compost, they worked very well. A few weeds grew up in the small spaces between the boxes and later beds made like this had a layer of cardboard under the boxes first to block out any weed growth.

Without a doubt the wood chips have been an amazing resource, but they have brought with them some problems in the shape of weeds. Somewhere in one of more of those loads were roots or seeds, or both, of bindweed, and as the wood has broken down and formed a deep layer of organic matter in the orchard area of the front garden, it has provided a rich and fertile space for the bindweed to grow. And grow it has!

There is far too much of it to be able to dig it out. The layer of chips is almost two feet (60cm) deep in some places and I would hazard a guess that it's completely riddled with bindweed roots. I will cover it with heavy duty plastic for the next two or three years, lifting it every few months to remove any roots I can see on the surface and then, hopefully I will be able to keep any remaining bindweed under control.

It has made me think again about using resources from off the site and about the importance of working towards a closed loop system, where all the resources for the garden come from the smallholding, to minimise the likelihood of contamination by external influences, like the bindweed.

Making a raised bed from cardboard boxes

CHICKENS OR DUCKS?

Chickens are often the entry level livestock for new homesteaders, smallholders, allotmenteers and gardeners and I understand the appeal of fresh eggs and the apparent ease of caring for them, but our experience leads me to believe that ducks are a much better option.

If you can look beyond the inevitable muddy patches that ducks seem to thrive upon making, they are much kinder to a productive area than chickens. A chicken will scratch at the ground, eat the plant and dig young plants out of the soil. Our chickens had little interest in eating slugs or snails, although they are quite partial to a tasty leather jacket or caterpillar. Ducks, on the other hand, do not scratch up the ground; they drill holes in it with their bills but, in the process, they manage to consume vast quantities of slugs and snails. Our large Aylesbury and Aylesbury x Pekin ducks are too heavy to fly, so tend to stay in their allotted areas, but chickens have no such manners and will fly, jump, squeeze and sneak their way into any space that they choose.

Ducks aren't always the brightest of creatures, but they brighten our day

Pet chickens (left to right): Bluebell, Jack, Diesel

Like most homesteaders, we got our first chickens shortly after moving here – three girls that were rehomed from my daughter's house. We took a crash course in chicken keeping and were quickly enamoured by the continuous supply of fresh eggs.

We then decided that we'd like blue coloured eggshells. We had fallen for the clever marketing in our local supermarket and imagined that these blue shelled eggs tasted better than those of the brown or white variety that we had bought in the past. With some experience, I now realise that it probably had more to do with what the birds were being fed or just that we had completely bought into the marketing messages.

I sourced some Crested Cream Legbar chickens from a gentleman who lived about 20 miles away. As luck would have it, he turned out to be one of the country's top breeders of these particular birds and we spent several afternoons in his company as he shared his memories of not only keeping the chickens, but of his life on the smallholding he shared with his wife. This handful of chickens were to be the first of very many, and ducks; I shall talk more about them later.

STARTING THE FOOD FOREST

The more I read and watched videos, the more I wanted to create a small food forest. I've seen several models; some have wood chips to keep the weeds down completely and others embrace the range of wildflowers and leafy weeds. I aimed at having a wood chips covered area, but over time the perennial weeds have crept back in and are once again taking over and I'm inclined to let them grow and just keep the pathways clear enough for us to walk through.

I started by sourcing some fruit trees. I had thought that I would need to spend £20-30 on each tree, but then I read that a supermarket chain was selling trees at less than £5 each. Mr J and I headed to the nearest store to see what the trees were like. They were probably not the quality in terms of shape and size that I would have chosen as ideal, but finances were tight and these cheap, bare-root trees gave me the opportunity to plant more trees than I had dared to hope for. We came home with 17 trees, a mixture of apple, pear, plum and cherry and over the next couple of weeks I planted them across the paddock. Although I had originally identified a small area to become a food forest, I quickly decided to look at the whole paddock as a food forest and have the vegetable garden surrounded by fruiting trees, shrubs and herbaceous plants. Four of those trees didn't survive the first winter, but the rest grew well and are thriving.

Jane once again came to help and we moved an apple tree from behind the greenhouse, where it was wedged between the greenhouse frame and the boundary fence. We planted it in the food forest, gave it a sturdy stake to help support it in the wind and it has grown happily there since.

I then planted shrubs and herbaceous perennials, annuals to self-seed and some climbers. We also made a small pond from old butyl liner that had been left here by the previous owners (or more likely, the owners before them) and some of the tree trunks from the sycamores that had been cut down. It wasn't intended to be a permanent fixture, but it still functions well and so has stayed. Along the fence leading to the gravel yard, I planted fruiting canes like tayberry and loganberry and nature has provided blackberries too.

To keep the cost of planting the food forest to a minimum, I bought one or two plants of each that I wanted and took cuttings from them. Currants root quickly and I soon built a stock of blackcurrants, redcurrants and white currants. I still had raspberries in pots that we had brought with us and those were planted in the ground, together with several large fruiting plants that friends had given to us.

I bought a set of 50 root cuttings of comfrey (the non-invasive Bocking 14) online, from the very lovely Ragmans Lane Farm, which I grew on in pots before adding them next to the fruit trees.

Bocking 14 comfrey, used for making compost tea, mulching
and for adding to the compost heap to provide trace minerals

MULTIFUNCTIONAL FENCING

When I created the pallet fence around the vegetable garden, I wanted to make sure that it would stay upright when the winds blew across the site, so I planned to place one pallet at a right angle to the main fence panels (made of pallets) every four or five pallets. As I started to build the fence it became obvious that I would need them every two pallets to give it the sturdiness and stability I wanted. Once I had put the supporting pallets in place, I could see something useful happening. I quickly changed my mind and put a pallet at a right angle between every pallet of fencing, creating a series of bays that would be ideal for making compost, or using for rainwater collection and storage.

The filled bays gave additional shelter from the wind and added stability to the structure. From inside the vegetable garden, I now had fencing to use for climbers that still gave the wildlife access across the garden and it wasn't too long before we met our resident hedgehog family.

As we acquired longer pallets, we swapped out the standard 4 feet (120cm) long pallets for the longer ones that had a more uniform look to them and reminded me more of fencing than pallets. The changing of

Compost bay fence around the vegetable garden

the pallets meant I had to adjust the position of the shorter stabilising pallets, but with a little careful manoeuvering I was able to keep the bays almost the same size.

Later on, I removed one of the pallets to create an additional entrance to the raised bed garden and put a metal arch there for climbing roses. I also placed a long pallet on top of the compost bay fence to create a work surface and fitted a double sink into it.

The sink had been found on Facebook Marketplace, free of charge. I used the sink upside down to draw a template on the work surface and cut out the necessary section to allow me to drop the sink into place. Using a Jubilee clip, I connected a garden hose to the water inlet pipe below the sink, and the other end can be attached to the stand-pipe in the garden. Buckets placed on the ground below the sinks allow me to catch the water as it drains out of the sink to use again in the garden. Once a bucket is full, I empty it into a water storage drum that I've put near the end of the work surface, which gives me quick access to water for watering the plants or compost heap.

PALLETS

Pallets are usually treated to destroy any parasites or insects in the wood. Pallets that are being sent internationally have to have a treatment stamp on them, which helps us to identify how they have been treated. There are treatment marks (two letters) specific to some countries and the most commonly used in the UK include:

DB Debarked. Most pallets are made from wood that has had the bark removed; this is done to ensure that any treatments will be applied efficiently to the wood.

HT Heat Treated. Pallet wood has been heated to at least 56°C (60°C for hardwoods) for a minimum of 30 minutes.

KD Kiln Dryed. Pests are killed off by heating pallets in a kiln. Kiln drying can also avoid other issues like warping and fungal growth. When a mill dries the wood to a higher temperature, it may also be marked as heat treated e.g. KD-HT.

DH Dielectric Heated. A method of heating a material using a high-frequency electromagnetic field.

MB Methyl Bromide. These pallets have been treated with a highly toxic pesticide. Do NOT use pallets marked with MB in the garden or burn them on a fire.

THE VULNERABLE GARDEN

It took a couple of years or more for the number of pests and predators to start to balance out. During the first year many of the brassicas ended up looking like lace doilies, peas and beans were covered in holes from bean beetles and the attacks by aphids seemed never ending.

I needed to find ways to protect the brassicas from cabbage white butterflies and cabbage moths (the caterpillars of which are green and can disguise themselves so well on the ribs of leaves).

Rummaging in one of the disused piggeries (a glamorous term for the crumbling outbuilding that was once home to pigs), I found some lengths of MDPE piping. Mr J cut it into lengths of approximately 6 feet (2m) and I pushed them into the ground on each side of a raised bed to form a tunnel. Online I searched for suitable netting, but decent quality butterfly netting was out of my price range. Although there was no particular set budget for this, I wanted to find the cheapest effective alternatives for everything I did. I spotted some scaffolding debris netting, which came in various widths and lengths, and I ordered 65ft (20m) of netting that was 6'6" (2m) wide. Debris netting is certainly close knit enough to keep out butterflies, but it does come with a reinforced section that has holes in it, presumably for securing it to scaffolding. Still, I figured that this was going to be better than no protection at all.

I secured some bamboo canes across the top of the piping arches with recycled baler twine and draped the netting over the skeletal structure, fixing

The caterpillars made huge holes in the cabbages leaving them filled with poo and unpleasant to deal with during meal preparations

it to the bamboo with more baler twine through the holes in the reinforced section. It wasn't perfect, but it worked – mostly! In later years I used the sewing machine to stitch a seam along the lengths of the debris netting which sealed the holes completely.

I weighed the netting down at ground level with pieces of wood and bricks to prevent it lifting in the wind and giving access to the unwanted visitors. Except they aren't unwanted, I don't want them to go, I want them here, all the butterflies and moths in their assorted colours and sizes, but I don't want them devouring the very food that I am growing for our consumption. There was a simple solution and one that has worked well.

In the vegetable garden I interplanted crops, carrots among kale, onions around salads and carrots, in the hope of disguising the smell of carrots from carrot root fly and also marigolds near beans to encourage pollinators to visit the beans.

To attract more pollinators and other insects, I sowed seeds of wildflowers, like cornflowers, flax and calendula, in module trays and planted them in the vegetable garden hoping that they would scatter their seeds to the winds and, to some extent, that they'd naturalise around the vegetable garden, in its pathways and along the pallet fence boundary. By far the most successful has been borage, which now seems to tiptoe the fine line between plentiful and a nuisance. Its beautiful star shaped flowers offer nectar for most months of the year in our garden. The calendula has also established itself, but as the plants are smaller and less prone to flopping all over the paths and blocking our way, they seem less obvious except for those few weeks each year that the garden is ablaze with bright orange flowers.

The more insects we had in the garden, the more insect predators were likely to arrive and their predators and so on. We wanted an abundance of wildlife, but for that to happen successfully, I needed to continue to provide the building blocks of an ecosystem upon which they could feed.

We were starting to see how quickly nature might find a balance. As we put in more plants and left areas to grow weeds like stinging nettles and brambles, we saw more and more wildlife.

Planting brassicas under netting to
protect them against the caterpillars
of cabbage white butterfly and
cabbage moth

Bees visit the flowers of this white
variety of borage much of the year

Blackberries grow in the hedgerows around Byther Farm

Painted Lady butterfly

FORAGING & THE POTENTIAL FOR ABUNDANCE

Given the slow pace at which we were developing the vegetable garden, I knew that we wouldn't have enough homegrown food to see us through the winter, so I looked at other ways to boost our supplies.

The fields around our smallholding are surrounded by hedges of blackthorn, hawthorn and blackberries, all of which hold potential for additional food and drink. I learnt that there is more than one type of blackberry; up to then I had thought that they were pretty much all the same, but it seems not. The earliest fruiting of the blackberry brambles offer big, plump, very juicy berries in late June and early July, while the later fruiting varieties have smaller, harder and less sweet berries.

I gather the early blackberries for eating, freezing whole and raw and for making jam and jelly. The later blackberries are gathered for making wine and cooked before freezing for use in blackberry and apple crumble and also in savoury dishes.

We started selling chicken eggs to local residents and as neighbours got to know about what we were trying to achieve, they offered us apples in exchange for eggs. People were delighted that

I was prepared to go and pick up the windfall apples and exchange them for eggs. Some neighbours just gave us a gift of apples and during the first year I prepared and stored what I thought were masses of apples. During our second year, friends were even more generous and I processed over 300lbs (135kg) of my favourite fruit for cooking. Many were made into apple sauce, even more were cooked and frozen, others I made into wine. It seemed like a vast quantity of apples, but within a year we had consumed them all. In much smaller quantities, we were also given plums.

As I began to harvest vegetables from the garden, I swapped some of our glut for foods that we hadn't grown. I had no success with courgettes (zucchini) the first year and my neighbour had failed to grow any runner beans. It was easy to exchange our surpluses and at the start of our second year I agreed with my neighbour that I would grow the beans for both houses and they would grow the courgettes (zucchini). It was a simple arrangement, but it worked very well.

FEAR OF FAILURE VS CONFIDENCE IN ABILITY

There are times when I wonder why I so glibly make huge, life-changing statements; 'I can grow most of our food' was one of them. In principle it's easy: we had land, I had some knowledge and experience, what could possibly go wrong?

Because I had no other source of income, I felt weighed down with the pressure of needing to provide us with food. Mr J had no such expectations; he was delighted with whatever had grown. I put that pressure on myself and there were times when I felt very insecure about the choice I had made and the commitment that I'd undertaken.

Above all else I was afraid of failing.

When I talked to Mr J about my worries, he reminded me that I had been very ill, that I was still recovering and that the pressure I felt was self-inflicted. He was (and continues to be) very good at planting my feet firmly back on solid ground.

It was probably a full year into this adventure before I started to believe that working alongside nature, I had the ability to do what was required for this land to produce enough food to sustain us. I needed to see how much food we had stored away as we were going into the first winter after creating the vegetable garden. Once I had seen the variety and quantity of food we had from just half the vegetable garden space, grown in a thin layer of soil on top of the poor quality

paddock, I gained some faith in my physical abilities and in the garden's ability to feed us.

By the end of the first year we had eaten fresh foods from the garden and had a small supply in the freezer including broad (fava) beans, cabbage, green runner beans, the white kidney type bean from inside runner beans, carrots and tomatoes. We also had foraged and gifted fruit, like blackberries and apples. In the ground for harvesting over winter were parsnips, kale and leeks. In storage we had onions, garlic and pumpkins which, it turned out, tasted awful. A vital lesson was learnt in the first year of growing squash – big may be beautiful, but it's the taste that matters.

A	Permanent planting of artichokes	21	Runner beans
10	Empty	20	Empty
9	Empty	19	Empty
8	Purple curly kale, bergamot	18	Empty
7	Beetroot, swede (rutabaga), January King cabbage	17	Empty
6	Leeks, squashes, lemon balm, parsley	16	Borlotti beans, squashes
5	Kale, rainbow chard, leeks	15	Peas, mangetout, carrots, cornflowers, flax
4	Perpetual spinach, carrots, purple sprouting broccoli, sunflowers	14	Parsnips
3	Squashes, potatoes, leeks	13	Onions/leeks, French beans, red cabbage, celery
2	Purple kale, January King cabbage, carrots, hollyhocks	12	Onions/curly kale, perpetual spinach, lettuce
1	Red onions, lettuce, carrots, beetroot/leeks	11	Garlic, broad (fava) beans/ French beans, leeks, kale, oca

The 'empty' sections are places where we haven't created the raised beds yet. Given that this was our first year here and that we were unable to rotavate the ground as we had anticipated, I am very pleased with how much we have achieved, especially as now I've realised that churning up the ground would have been a bad decision. I've learnt a great deal about the garden, the way wind blows throughout the year, the sunniest spots, the driest places and the subtle slope of the site.

The appalling soil that we started with is already improving having added tons of compost made in our compost bins and bays, wood chippings, well-rotted horse manure and topsoil. The health of the soil life is improving too; it now has masses of worms, bugs of various kinds, fungi and bacteria.

The chickens have played their part in improving the soil by scratching at the surface of the ground and fertilising it as they go. Their used bedding materials have gone into the compost heaps and into the circles of love, which in turn have gone into the ground. Even the young chicks have been working hard in the garden.

Excerpt from 16th September 2016

PETS

Our much loved cat, Monty

A full year after moving here, we were joined by two rescue cats, Tabitha and Monty. They had been much loved by their former owners, but they had died, leaving the two elderly cats without a place to live. We were very happy to offer the two pedigree British Shorthaired cats a home for the rest of their lives. The cat adoption agency told us that the pair were inseparable, but once they had settled into the rhythm of life on the smallholding, they were very definitely, totally and utterly separable. They fought, spat, scratched and fought some more. They both displayed signs of stress and after a year or so, Tabitha's incontinence became so severe, that we and the vet felt her quality of life had deteriorated to the point of it being unfair to prolong her life.

It was a truly horrid week when we said goodbye to Tabitha. And then it seemed that life was kicking us when we were down because the very next day, Mrs Warne injured her hip so badly that I had to put her out of her misery.

The lounge had been Tabitha's territory and until Monty had the house to himself, he had avoided being in the room at all. Over the course of two weeks, he gingerly sniffed at the air in the lounge and then ran back outside, then he got brave enough to go into the room for a couple of moments and eventually he made his way onto the sofa and snuggled up next to me as I watched television. Monty has been my almost constant companion ever since.

That's not strictly true; when Mr J is at work Monty is my companion, following me to the garden each time I go. When Mr J comes home, it's as though I don't exist and he follows Mr J around for a couple of hours, even sitting in a spare chair in the study.

Our neighbours also have cats.

Monty has an odd relationship with them. Almost every night Monty can be found yowling, screaming and fighting tooth and claw with one of the cats from next door. Most nights I put on my shoes and a coat and pad outside to break up the fight and tell Monty to come home. Looking slightly embarrassed, he wanders back into the house and shoves his face into his food bowl. Each morning he then heads down the lane to the same neighbour's home to pay his friends a visit. It's almost as though he's asking them if they can come out to play.

Monty quickly learnt to give the chickens a wide berth. They were not interested in having him around them and he, in turn, seemed rather wary of them. Equally with the ducks, a respectful distance is kept, but he can often be seen keeping watch over them as they

Day-old ducklings are transferred from the incubator to the brooder and nursery pen

dibble through the undergrowth and pathways of the garden. Newly hatched chicks and ducklings, however, are of great interest. Even before the young birds have hatched from their eggshells, Monty can be found sitting on a chair near the incubator as if waiting to greet them. Once we have taken them out of the incubator, he likes to have a look at the baby birds.

He doesn't seem interested in chasing them or even 'feeling' them with a paw; he just watches, slightly mesmerised by the tiny new birds with their high-pitched cheeps and squeaks. So far, each batch of young birds has had a furry guardian. Monty seems to check them on a regular basis and sits near them in their nursery pen. I wouldn't trust him on his own with the young birds in the open, but in their nursery run, he seems nothing but parental towards them.

On the few occasions that a chicken has hatched some young and we've let them free-range with the mother, Monty steers clear of them. I suspect he has had a warning peck or two from a broody mother hen and has learnt his lesson. Mother hens may look all fluffed up and pretty, but they guard their young quickly and fiercely!

Like so many other animals, Monty seems to sense when we or the poultry are not feeling well. and one summer I separated a Brahma chicken from the flock. I put her on a towel in the kitchen doorway, where I hoped she could find some peace and quiet. Within minutes, Monty had appeared and settled down next to her where he remained until she quietly slipped away. Moments after she had died, he got up and went back out into the garden to resume his sleep.

HARVESTING AND STORING – FREEZING

I wish I could say that the first year of growing was a roaring success. It wasn't an entire failure; we had plenty of food, but not necessarily the variety of taste and textures to make interesting eating all year round. I learnt that growing enough food to feed us for the year was a very different beast to growing a few vegetables to supplement our diet.

If I was going to grow the majority of our food and make a success of it, I would need to plant a wider variety of vegetables than I had grown in the past and get to grips with how to spread the burden of harvesting and storage. So much seemed to be ready all at once and far from spending my time preparing meals, it felt like a race to just get everything stored away so I could make meals at a later date.

I was getting too tired, too often.

I have SAD (Seasonal Affective Disorder) and during the winter I find doing very much on a practical level really difficult. In the past I had ensured that during autumn I filled the freezer with meals that simply needed to be defrosted and reheated to provide us with nutritious filling food. By late autumn I was starting to wind down for the winter and I hadn't managed to prepare many homemade ready meals for the freezer, although it was chock-a-block full of ingredients to make those meals.

The freezer was so full that we decided to buy a second one and because I didn't want the running costs of a large chest freezer that wasn't filled up, I chose a smaller chest freezer.

As the harvesting continued, I filled it within 48 hours.

We searched adverts on local sites and notice boards and found another medium size freezer.

To save on electricity I am careful about rotating the food in the freezers. When stocks start getting low, I transfer all the food into one freezer and turn one off completely, making the now full freezer run more efficiently and saving on power.

Another arrangement that works well for us is our kitchen etiquette. On days that Mr J is at work, he rises much earlier in the day than me and on those days he cooks breakfast for himself. Many evenings we eat 'nibbles' of fruit, veg, cheese or cold meats with relishes and chutneys. Our main meal of each day is cooked and almost always by me. From the start of our relationship, I asked Mr J not to interfere in the kitchen space while I'm cooking and he has kindly respected my request. This division of labour works well for us both.

I love cooking and often lose myself in the creative process so much that I'm not necessarily aware of anyone in close proximity. It would be all too easy to turn around with a knife in my hand or a pan of scalding hot water and bump into him. If the kitchen area is a cook-only zone, then accidents are much less likely to happen.

Beet leaves   beetroot (beets)   Brussels sprouts
cabbage   carrots   celery   celeriac
chard   kale   kalettes   leeks   lettuce
oca   parsnips   pea shoots   rhubarb   root parsley
purple sprouting broccoli   salad leaves   salsify
bay   borage flowers   chives   dill
fennel   garlic leaves   lemon balm   marjoram
mint   parsley   rosemary   thyme   wild garlic   winter savory

Harvesting carrots

YEAR TWO

2017

NATURE JUST WANTS TO GROW

From the kitchen windows we have great views of colourful sunsets

EXPANDING THE POTENTIAL, CONSOLIDATING THE START

For the last 30 years or so, by autumn each year I start feeling low. As the light levels drop and the daylight hours become shorter, I slowly slide into a depression. My mood drops and my body slows down and somewhere between November and Christmas I grind almost to a halt, sleeping for great swathes of the day. It's more than a touch of the winter blues, it's a deep-seated low-grade ache that overtakes my brain and body leaving me with the feeling of being unable to move properly. As my movements slow down and everything becomes an exhausting effort, I usually describe it as feeling like I am wading through waist high jelly.

The slow down begins just at the time when the harvesting is at a peak and I need to be in the kitchen preparing food for storage. Luckily, I find the process of chopping, peeling, cooking and preparing food relaxing, enjoyable and incredibly satisfying and this helps me work through the tasks at a reasonable pace.

I used to fight this state of being, punishing myself mentally for being so 'weak', which only made it worse. Many moons ago I sought help from the medical services and with the help of a mental health nurse, I found a pathway through the fog of SAD that works for me. One of the tools that I use is having a project.

I like projects; I like the sense of purpose and achievement that they bring. During those winter months, when so much seems utterly hopeless, I use very small projects to keep me going. Some of the best projects have been the ones where I put pen to paper and make plans for the following year. This allows my imagination to run riot and my mind to focus on warmer days filled with activity rather than the grey damp days of a British winter. For the last three years, those small projects have also included creating videos. The self-imposed discipline of creating videos on a regular basis has, on occasions, been really tough and I've slowly learnt not to beat myself up emotionally if I haven't been able to finish (or even start) a video on time.

Winter is also the time that, like so many others, I tend to pile on the weight. Having already reached the heaviest I'd ever been, I told myself it was okay to eat what I liked, that I could lose the weight in the spring when I felt better and so, yet again, the pounds crept on and my body started to hurt with the burden of carrying extra weight around.

It took a long time to learn that this state of depression during the winter is a transient thing, that as the daylight hours increased, I would, most likely, naturally lift from the funk I was in and would return to feeling like me again. I also discovered light boxes. Recommended by the nurse that I was seeing, I use a light box as the daylight hours start to dwindle. To get maximum benefit from it, I should really start using it in the middle of August, but the last thing I want to think about doing during the long, warm August days is to sit in front of a bright light to top up my serotonin levels. Although I don't necessarily notice the positive effects of using the light box, those around me can tell when I haven't used it for long or often enough.

With less to do outdoors, winter seemed like a good time to study and to increase my understanding of the garden systems and that of the world around me. I watched endless hours of videos online, but reading was more difficult to do. As my hypothyroidism had developed and levels of vitamins and minerals that I absorbed dropped, my vision had become poorer and reading made my eyes hurt and often I just couldn't concentrate. I had stacks of books that I wanted to read, hungry for the pearls of wisdom and information they contained, so I developed the pattern of reading for 15 to 20 minutes and then going into the kitchen and staring out of the window for a while, looking at the trees in the distance to rest my eyes from the close-up work they had been doing and it worked! I could read, rest, watch videos, repeat and bit by bit over the winter and early spring months I had learnt, researched and absorbed masses of information.

That winter was an odd one; although I felt low, I also experienced an underlying sense of satisfaction and felt calmer than I had for many winters beforehand; I was beginning to work with the seasons, to allow myself to rest at a time when there was less to do outside, and to recuperate. By giving myself permission to slow down, I felt less guilt which in turn made me feel better, more relaxed and with fewer really low dips in my mood. It would be another year before I fully realised that I was working with the seasons at such a deep level, but something inside me was shifting; my mindset was changing.

NATURAL LINKS

There have been moments when I've been struck by the perfect simplicity or the unspoken symmetry of how things fit together. Seeing the links between the elements, plants, soil and wildlife allows us to support their relationships in a positive way.

Watching many videos on YouTube inspired me to think carefully about how I could create an edible landscape at Byther Farm and how it might fit within our space. I then took a step back to look at the wider picture here and realised that rather than create a food forest within our smallholding, most of our 0.8 acre could be the food forest. It was a small shift in perspective, but one that has had a huge impact for how I work with the land. Gone was the necessity to neatly segregate different types of plants: annuals in one area, trees in another, shrubs and perennials somewhere else. In fact, combining the plants into groups, guilds, had distinct advantages as one plant could support and enhance the growth of another, I found it more aesthetically pleasing and it didn't fight against my slightly messy nature and dislike of rigid, regimented lines within the garden. Reading and research added yet more information and inspiration and some understanding of planting distances that I might need for the food forest to work in our temperate climate.

Planting for the long term doesn't do much to satisfy the urge for instant gratification and as a result of wanting some instant impact, I've enjoyed using mature shrubs, annuals and short-lived perennial plants to add height, shape and colour in the garden.

WHAT GROWS WHERE

We started the year with four or five raised beds filled with weeds and I became disheartened at the amount of time it took to clear them before I could start growing any food in them. I promised myself that I would not go into another winter with beds filled with weeds and that this year I would ensure I kept on top of the pernicious weeds in the raised beds. I might stay inside and rest for much of the winter, but the weeds carry on growing, albeit slowly, and I didn't want to start the next year with the same uncomfortable feeling of failure.

This is one of my favourite photographs taken by Mr J

There are plants that I love to grow, but I don't necessarily like them to eat. In a productive garden these are essentially ornamental plants. I'm happy to grow ornamentals, especially if they have the added value of attracting pollinators, but they can't be the mainstay of the vegetable garden that's supposed to be providing for the family.

One of the key things that I have had to learn is that it's more important to grow what we eat than grow things that I like because of their aesthetics.

Changing my thinking has been one of the hardest things. In previous gardens vegetables were grown in a cottage garden style and added to the overall look. Here I have a dedicated growing area and although it can look nice, its primary role is food production.

I started by growing those that take the least mental effort, but quickly realised that we wouldn't want to eat a highly restricted diet of just a few types of vegetables for the rest of our lives – it was time to make a list.

We thought about all the vegetables that we know we like and then I researched which ones I hadn't grown before that would be likely to grow easily in our climate. Narrowing down our vegetable wish-list helped to make the task ahead seem less daunting.

Once we'd done that, I then expanded that list by looking at different varieties of familiar vegetables. For example, I had grown runner beans many times, so I knew how to grow beans and I looked for other types of beans that I could grow to give us more variety. In our second year here, as with the first, I grew White Lady runner beans. I've liked this variety for many years; it has a creamy white flower and the bean inside the pod has a white skin (rather than red and black like most runner beans). I also expanded our bean selection to include Greek Gigantes beans (which have become our new go-to bean for filling, hearty meals), Borlotti beans (which I first had on holiday in France and have since discovered that I prefer them fresh to frozen) and 'The Prince' French beans which are sweet and juicy and a delight in salads as well as hot meals.

I continued exploring the options of new varieties of plants that I knew how to grow. I then chose a few from our list that I hadn't grown before. As I understand the basics of growing and work on the basis that nature just wants to grow, trying to grow a new vegetable isn't a daunting process. More than anything I just don't want to have a crop fail completely as it's such a waste of time, energy, resources and space in the garden.

We've also had to change some of our eating habits.

Before we moved here and we were both working in managerial roles, I cooked regularly, but often I used pre-packaged foods and occasionally pre-prepared vegetables. We also ate whatever we fancied from the range of fruit and vegetables on offer at the supermarket rather than eating what was in season.

As more and more of the food on our table was coming from the garden, we slowly exchanged 'fresh' fruit that had been flown half the way around the world for apples, pears, plums and cherries from our own trees that had been frozen or stored in the barn or soft fruits like strawberries, raspberries and elderberries that had been frozen whole, ready to be defrosted and eaten either cooked or raw (but not the elderberries; they need to be cooked before consumption).

The same applied to vegetables and there were several that we could harvest fresh from the garden in the winter months. The main-stay of our carb type vegetables were no longer potatoes, but parsnips and frozen beans.

Caterpillars of the peacock butterfly on stinging nettles

A PLACE FOR NATURE

Having put in the hedges around the perimeter, I had thought that beneath the hedgerow I would put all the larger stones that I found in the garden to get them out of the way and to create hiding places for wildlife. I also guessed that the weeds would move in and increase the diversity around the edges of the gardens. That has happened to some extent; I didn't move as many stones as I had imagined I would and the weeds aren't as diverse as I thought they might be, but it's still early days and as the hedging plants mature they will have an impact on the life living in and around them.

We also decided to have some patches in different places across the site that we'd leave untended and allow stinging nettles to grow in them, in particular to support the butterfly and moth species that thrive on them, like the peacock butterfly. What I didn't anticipate was that over time great swathes of land would become engulfed in a stinging nettle, dock and bramble tangle creating an almost impenetrable barrier and in other places the combination varies (bindweed, cinquefoil and hogweed), but the effect is the same. I feel as though I wobble along a pathway between rejoicing in letting

nature do what it does best and feeling utterly overwhelmed by the jungle it is creating.

I admire stinging nettles. They are efficient propagators and defend themselves with their painful leaves and stems. I know that stinging nettles are a nutrient dense crop, but we don't like the taste of them at all and neither the chickens nor ducks seem to like them either, so the best use for them is to create compost and compost tea with them. As long as I can cut them before they start to go to seed then I can add them to the compost heaps without spreading them even further around the smallholding. However, stinging nettles grow fastest at the time of year when I am busiest in the garden and as yet, I haven't managed to cut them back before they start flowering.

The row of old fruit trees in the far end of the duck enclosure shows evidence of having been home to much wildlife. I'm not quite sure what keeps the tallest plum tree upright and for a long time we thought it was dead. The damsons and wild plums had blossomed and started to turn green with new leaves before the plum tree showed any signs of life. It is gnarly and battered; parts of it are dead and riddled with woodworm holes and a hole in the trunk shows where squirrels have lived in it, leaving dozens of empty nutshells as evidence.

Every year, the old plum tree has produced some fruit, but usually it is so high up in the canopy that I can't reach most of it. The fruit ripens on the branches and falls to the ground with a splat where wasps and other insects pick off the fruit flesh leaving the ground scattered with plum stones like little pebbles on a beach.

Apparently ducks also like plums.

Each morning in late summer, when I let the ducks out of their houses, they have a drink, snatch a mouthful or two of food and then make a beeline for the trees. I know whenever they have found another plum from the delighted sounds that they make and I know when they can't find any more plums to hoover up, because they wander back to their pond to wash off the sticky plum juice from around their bills and their feathers.

There is a point each year when the plums are very ripe, over-ripe, and almost start to ferment before they fall off the trees. The ducks seem to like these the most. We have wondered whether these fermenting plums make the ducks slightly drunk and whether that is why they waddle quite so much?

WHAT IS EASY VS WHAT FEELS RIGHT

Faced with head-high stinging nettles and thickets of brambles I can understand why people are tempted to, and indeed do, turn to chemical warfare on their weeds. But that's not an option for us; we have made the decision to work with nature, not against it. The sprays, potions and lotions that contain a cocktail of chemicals are not what we want for the land that we live on.

Both Mr J and I have said that on occasions we feel daunted, overwhelmed and depressed by the amount of work there is to do in the garden, to keep the weeds under control.

What we needed was another mindset shift.

We needed a change in how we look at the unwanted vegetation and to stop making value judgements about their aesthetic beauty or role in our garden based on our expectations that come from the neat and tidy gardens of our childhoods. Those gardens had manicured lawns, with edges clipped to give a sharp line, and no plant was in the wrong place. No wonder it is hard to see how a scruffy patch of 'stingers' fits into the scheme.

My parents' garden was no different. I recall Dad spending, seemingly, hours walking back and forth across the lawn with his trusty old Atco petrol mower in front of him. It almost pulled him along as it cut the grass, spitting the clippings into the grass box, the built-in roller gently coaxing the grass to lie in one direction. The result of his to-ing and fro-ing was, to my young eyes, a magically stripy lawn. He would then rake up any grass clippings that had spilt (or get one of my brothers to do it) and he'd neaten the edges of the borders with a half moon or long handled edging shears. It was all very neat, but it also made me feel a bit uncomfortable at the tidiness of it all.

Then, at some point in the 1970s, my father bought a Flymo hover mower. Its blade whizzed round in circles on the horizontal plane rather than being a cylinder blade like his previous mower. I can still recall the feeling of lightness and relief when I saw that the lawn was now cut in swirls and patterns and, best of all, that some of the grass got left on the lawn as it was being cut. I think from an early age I was destined to be a relaxed-style gardener.

There is a difference between being a chaotic, messy gardener and a 'working with nature' one. I have chosen to not over-tidy some areas of the garden to provide a habitat for a more diverse range of wildlife. Unfortunately, I am also a fairly messy gardener too! All too often I start working in one area and get distracted and wander off to another area. The effect is that the gardens often look unfinished or abandoned and indeed they are, but over the course of the growing year, all the tasks are, more or less, completed and to the casual observer's eye it may look like chaos, but to me it's a delightful, fulfilling, constant work in progress.

The basic practicalities may be tiresome to get organised, but in the long run, are time-savers and good practice.

Storing hand tools in an upturned pallet keeps them tidy and close to where they will be used

One of my worst habits is to leave the few tools that I use lying around and then I cannot find them when I next want to use them. After yet another afternoon wasted as we searched for a missing hoe, Mr J suggested that I keep all the tools in a central location and I now use one pallet in the vegetable garden fence to store the larger hand tools. From their secure home I can access them easily from whichever part of the garden I am working in. From a health and safety viewpoint, keeping the tools with blades or sharp edges in a secure place is good practice. I still haven't found a good place to keep trowels and hand forks, although I am getting better at placing them at the end of raised beds so that they are visible at a quick glance.

THE RIGHT TOOL FOR THE JOB

I don't have a huge number of tools for the homestead; sometimes I wish I had more gadgets and gizmos, but I also see no point in having more stuff just for the sake of it.

During the first year I had become increasingly frustrated at the lack of mobility of our power tools as they all needed to be plugged into the mains electricity supply. We decided to invest in some battery powered tools, like a screwdriver, drill and jigsaw. Having a mobile tool kit opened up a new range of possibilities and I practised some very basic woodwork skills.

Although I now have a few more tools, I think the most important pieces of equipment for use on our smallholding are appropriate clothing and a handful of basic tools.

Essentials:

- ▶ Protective footwear, gloves, hat, waterproof trousers, sun hat, and jacket or coat (my coats are all equipped with a pair of gloves and some baler twine), protective eye goggles.

- ▶ Scissors, secateurs (snips), wire cutters, trowel, hand fork, hoe, border spade, border fork, rake.

- ▶ Screwdriver, drill, jigsaw, pallet breaker, hammer, tape measure, mallet, lump hammer, hand saw, spirit level, stapler.

As well as the tools, there are some other things that I feel are essentials for our homestead. Among the most important are compost and soil building or soil supporting materials in their many forms and water collection facilities.

OFF-SITE COMPOSTING MATERIALS

Moving to a site with seemingly so little potential for creating compost, I looked at local sources for organic materials with which to make some. During our first year I had sourced spent grain from a local brewery and mixed it with straw purchased at a local farm. The grain was given to us free of charge in exchange for some chicken eggs. In hindsight I may not have done things quite as they should be; I think (but I'm not certain) that I may have had to register as a disposal site for a waste product, but I didn't know about this possible requirement. If it's an option that you are interested in doing on a large scale, it's worth checking out the local regulations. This was a quick, if somewhat smelly, way to make large amounts of compost.

Spent brewery grain, if not mixed with adequate amounts of brown materials, will ferment and start to decompose and it will stink. I can only describe the aroma as smelling of vomit. It's like being shut in an enclosed space with huge amounts of sick; it's grim to say the least! But, if mixed with enough brown material, it will quickly break down without filling the air with its unpleasant smell.

I layered straw and spent brewery grain in a heap and once it had started to produce some heat in the centre of it, I made small pockets in the top of the heap, filled them with topsoil and planted some squash in them. I had to keep an eye on the moisture level in the heap and water it regularly because the open nature of the heap, with so much straw in it, allowed water to drain away very quickly. The warmth of the materials composting and then the nutrients they provided gave us a good pumpkin harvest.

I also experimented with using straw packed into pallets to make insulated compost bays. I found the composting material broke down quickly, but I'm not sure it was any faster than in the compost heaps without the insulation. One day I shall do a more measured experiment.

I then agonised over whether bringing straw from non-organic sources was a good idea; I looked for a local source of organic straw, but failed to find any and since then I haven't bought more. It seems to me that depending on where I look for answers about the safety of using non-organic straw in the garden, the answers I find are very different.

I also had a seemingly endless supply of wood chips and wood shavings and at times I wondered whether we would be able to make use of the sheer volume of wood chips that we had delivered by the tree surgeon. Over time, the deliveries have reduced and I've declined the offer of more on occasions abut we have been able to make use of all that has been delivered.

Layering straw and spent brewery grain made a hot bed for growing squashes, while also creating compost

Packing straw into the spaces of a pallet and a covering over the compost made an insulated compost heap

ON SITE COMPOSTING MATERIALS

The main sources of organic materials on site are leaves from the huge sycamore trees by the piggeries, bedding from the chicken and duck houses, annual weeds and kitchen peelings. For the first two autumns I used the leaves in compost heaps and since then I have used them to make leaf mould. Leaf mould is easy to make; it just takes time. Unlike a compost heap, the leaves are broken down slowly by fungal action, replicating the process that happens on a woodland floor. A pile of leaves, some moisture and time results in a fine, dark crumbly material that is good for using in a potting compost mixture and ideal as a mulch around plants.

I don't chop the leaves before putting them into the container because I don't want to potentially damage any caterpillars spending the winter among the leaves. The sycamore trees are home to some of the UK's hairiest caterpillars. The sycamore moth caterpillar, *Acronicta aceris*, has orange hairs and a row of white dots with black edges along its back. For such a colourful caterpillar the moth is a drab affair, grey, grey-brown and cream. I've also found other caterpillars like the Knot Grass Moth which I am careful not to damage on our smallholding.

USING ANIMAL BEDDING

We use a chopped rapeseed straw (and occasionally chopped miscanthus) for the poultry bedding. The used bedding from the duck house can be put directly onto the soil as a mulch because duck faeces has a high water content and is mild. During the autumn and winter, I clean out the duck house twice a week which gives me plenty of mulching material for the raised beds and it composts in situ, breaking down over the next year or so.

Used chicken bedding on the other hand, must be left to mellow and compost before it can be used in the garden as it has the potential to burn the stems of plants. The potentially high alkalinity of chicken faeces means that generally it is less suitable to use around acid-loving plants like blueberries. As part of a healthy mix in our compost heaps, I have found no problems using chicken bedding to increase the organic matter in our soil.

I have also used chicken bedding as a mulch over larger areas in the garden that are empty over winter. Spread out over the area in autumn, it hasn't completely broken down by spring, but the action of the rain on the bedding means that it isn't as 'hot' on the plant stems as I feared

Two-year-old leaf mould

MAKING LEAF MOULD

Gather fallen leaves into a heap, moisten with water and leave them for 12 months or more. To contain the leaves and stop them being blown around you can place them into a suitable container. A circle made from chicken wire works well; I use some pallets strapped together or you can use plastic bags with several holes punched into them to make sure the leaves don't become waterlogged. A pile of leaves that start out at three feet high will end up as just a few inches of leaf mould.

No other materials, like nitrogen-rich grass clippings, are added to the heap as it is a long, slow, cool process; adding green materials would produce a compost rather than leaf mould, both very useful, but different end products.

To speed up the process of making leaf mould, you can chop up the leaves by running a lawn mower over them a few times or passing through a shredder before putting them into the heap. It is worth checking the leaves before you start to make sure that no wildlife, like hedgehogs, are asleep in the leaves.

it might be and I've generally used these areas to grow (alkaline preferring) brassicas in for the first year after mulching.

I've also used nettles and comfrey in the compost heaps to increase the amount of green materials in the heap and add nutrients. And we make liquid fertiliser – compost tea – from the nettles and comfrey. I make a very basic plant feed by putting either stinging nettles or comfrey or both, into an old pillowcase, tying some string or baler twine around it to create a giant teabag and then plunging it into a container of water. Wait two to three weeks, agitating it occasionally, and then it's ready to use. It needs to be diluted before use – about one part compost tea to ten parts water.

I use a small water butt (sourced via the local Freecycle group) for making compost tea as it has a tap near the base and allows me to draw off some of the solution without having to touch it. It's strong smelling stuff and if accidentally splashed or spilt, the aroma seems to stay on the skin for days. Many different types of compost tea can be made and it's something I will be exploring more over the next year or two with help from videos, courses and books. I now have a copy of *Compost Teas for the Organic Grower* by Eric Fisher (Permanent Publications), which explains the process and potential for making compost teas and it's one of those books that I will no doubt dip in and out of, time and time again.

> Avoid splashing compost tea onto your skin or clothes; the strong smell can linger.

As comfrey grows so quickly and is superb for adding nutrients to the soil, I've used it in teas and have also harvested armfuls of it to mulch below trees and shrubs; they break down quickly, adding nutrients to the soil wherever they are put. This would also work using nettles although so far, I have only used them in the compost heaps.

FEEDING THE SOIL, FEEDING THE SOUL

The saying goes that 'nature abhors a vacuum' (Aristotle) and applied to gardening it translates into 'if you leave a patch of soil bare, nature will cover it with weeds'. There are many good reasons that this happens, like seeds being exposed to light that triggers them to germinate, and if left uncovered, soil is vulnerable to rain and wind erosion, so nature covers it with weeds to ensure that the roots hold the soil together and shade it from the effects of the elements. Mulching goes a long way to covering bare soil and protecting it from erosion and saving us from hours of removing unwanted weeds.

After just one year of building soil in the first ten raised beds in the vegetable garden I could see some progress in the quality of the soil

and soil life. Worms had returned, together with lots of beetles and in the areas that were as yet uncultivated, there were plenty of grass-hoppers and insects. Some larger animals had arrived: shrews, voles and field mice. The numbers of wild birds were starting to increase too. All signs that some of the things we were doing were right for the local wildlife population.

Among acres of monoculture farm fields, our plot had the makings of a haven, an oasis, for a diversity of wildlife.

I was unable to make compost fast enough to fill the raised beds that we created in the second year and so I turned to using part-composted wood chips in the beds to stretch the small amount of compost that we did have.

I half-filled a bed with part-composted wood chips and then made deep furrows in it, creating mounded rows of wood chips and then filled the spaces between with compost and planted into the compost.

It's not a practice I'd recommend on a large scale, but it worked enough to allow me to grow some food while I was waiting for the wood chips to break down. Three years later those beds are filled with rich black and crumbly soil that is high in organic matter and easy to work with.

Furrows made in wood chips to fill a raised bed

Rows of wood chips and compost in a raised bed

WHEN IS A WEED NOT A WEED?

My parents' garden was one of neat orderliness. Annual bedding was planted out in neat, straight rows. One of my father's favourites was a red salvia which, planted in regimented fashion in their front garden, reminded me of soldiers on parade.

I think it's fair to say that my garden is neither neat nor orderly and by design I don't plant out bedding plants in straight rows. Growing up, I imagined my garden to be chock-a-block filled with billowing flowers, all scrambling together to form a tapestry of colours, scents and textures. I admired the cottage gardens of Gertrude Jekyll, Rosemary Verey and Christopher Lloyd's Great Dixter garden and wanted the same free-form flow of foliage and flowers.

It was only when I started growing vegetables that I started to put plants in straight rows because that allowed me to assess quickly what was my potential harvest and what was a weed and then to hoe or hand weed between the rows. But that soon became a problem too.

Those tiny plants that were springing up between my rows of vegetables were technically weeds, as in they were plants in the wrong place, but some of them were also plants that I wanted to grow. Around 20 years or so ago I stopped hoeing the spaces between rows of plants until after I checked them carefully for seedlings of plants that I could transplant or pot up. It makes weeding the beds a more time-consuming activity, but the joy of discovering a new plant that I do want makes it worth the effort.

In our first spring here I bought and sowed seeds of the pheasant berry, *Lycesteria formosa*, but I could have just waited. By summer, seedlings were popping up all over the gravel yard and in the raised beds we had created. I lifted them carefully and transplanted them and each year I now give away dozens of them to friends and people from neighbouring villages.

Since then I have taken to leaving the 'weed' seedlings in situ, unless the plants are likely to end up too large for the place in which they are growing. It means that more and more often I have raised beds of poly-cultures as the self-sown vegetables grow where they have germinated. It took me a little while to feel comfortable with leaving a vegetable seedling to grow wherever it had germinated, but this way the beds have greater diversity in them each year and crops are less vulnerable to attack from a particular pest when there are other species of plants growing around them.

Lycesteria formosa, the Himalayan honeysuckle. The fully ripe berries are enjoyed by the birds, and may also be used in the kitchen.

SOURCING PLANTS

Driven by wanting to produce as much of our food as possible with limited financial resources, I prefer to grow many plants from seed and also propagate plants as much as possible.

When we bought some currant bushes at the local garden centre for the food forest, I chose several different varieties, but only one plant of each because I planned to propagate more of them from cuttings. Each year during the late summer and early autumn I have taken cuttings to steadily increase the number of plants.

There are varieties that I prefer to others, like blackcurrant Big Ben with its very tasty, huge, sweet fruit. Some varieties of currants have been bred to be very upright in habit, which is great for smaller

Big Ben is my favourite variety of blackcurrant

spaces, but I find harvesting the fruit trickier; I like the slightly more open shape of this variety. There are now several young plants waiting in pots to form a new hedge between the vegetable garden and the duck enclosure. They will be sheltered by the pallet fence from the winds and the ducks, who would strip them of fruit very quickly given half a chance and in turn, over the years, they will help to provide more shelter to the vegetable garden.

Some of the perennial vegetables were started from seed and have since been lifted and divided to provide us with additional plants. The rhubarb and globe artichokes are prime candidates for this.

PEST CONTROL, PREDATORS AND INTERVENTION

Inevitably, after I've planted vegetables and fruit in the garden, insects and other pests have arrived to feast on them. Having decided to work with nature as much as possible, I knew that I would have to learn appropriate ways to deal with pests as they arrived. I have never sprayed any edibles with pesticides, but I did use slug pellets. When we moved here and wanted to grow the healthiest food that we could, I had a rethink about their use. However irritating it is that slugs and snails seem to pop up from nowhere and devour young plants, I realised that if I poisoned the slugs, then I could also be poisoning the very animals that eat slugs; and that seemed counter-productive.

I took a multi-pronged approach to dealing with our one-footed friends. I start most of the annual vegetables in seed trays in the greenhouse, raised up on staging away from the immediate eyesight of slugs and snails and I grow them to a fairly good size before planting them out. My hope is that if a slimy pest does get to the plant that it won't eat so much of it that the plant is destroyed.

I tried making beer traps from milk bottles, which worked to some extent, but didn't seem to make a big impact in the onslaught of silvery trails across the garden. By far the most effective defence against slugs and snails, has been the keeping of ducks.

During late autumn, winter and early spring I allow the ducks to roam in the vegetable garden and food forest. They merrily spend their days foraging in the wood chip pathways and, to some extent, in the raised beds. I shut them out of the vegetable garden at the end of April as I start to put in the young plants and allow them to continue to forage in the food forest. I then shut them into their own enclosure as the currant bushes start to form fruit, or the ducks would strip the bushes of food that we want to harvest and store.

It's not a perfect arrangement and I have to net any beds that have crops in them while the ducks are in the vegetable garden as they too are partial to brassicas and onion leaves, but it does make a noticeable difference.

I've also noticed that as the wild bird population has increased in the garden, there seem to be fewer slugs and snails attacking the plants that we want to eat. It seems that slowly there is some balance coming to the garden.

Aphids can be a nuisance, blackfly looks unsightly on broad (fava) beans and their sticky secretions make the elderberry tree look sooty,

Sacrifice brassicas support cabbage
white butterfly and cabbage moth
caterpillars

but given a little time the ladybirds arrive and start to take control of
the aphid numbers. 2017 was the year of the ladybirds. Newspapers
reported 'invaders from far off shores' and they arrived in our garden
in their droves. Plants seemed to be covered in them, the fence posts
were a resting place for hundreds of them and the aphids seemed to
disappear in a matter of days. As I understand it, there is an annual
influx of Harlequin ladybirds, but this year seemed to bring more than

usual. I quietly wished that the numbers of ladybirds had been the same in the following years, but nevertheless, there are usually enough ladybirds to deal with the vast majority of aphids that find our garden.

After my disastrous attempt at growing cabbages in the first year, the low tunnels that I created for brassicas, covered with debris netting, worked like a charm with only the occasional unwanted visitor making it into the tunnels to find the brassicas.

I decided to plant 'sacrifice' brassicas, a selection of cabbages and kale grown in the open upon which the butterflies and moths can lay their eggs. I don't expect to be able to eat them and leave them through the winter to rot down in situ. This arrangement seems to work well, although if you asked a butterfly, I'm sure it would say it would rather I left all the brassicas in the open.

Mullein moth caterpillar is often considered a pest, but they are welcome here

I know that there are organic sprays that can be used on brassicas to help prevent further attack by butterflies and I'm told that it works very well, but it's not for us. I don't want to kill off cabbage white butterfly or cabbage moth, if anything I would like to see more of them. I have seen people wince when I tell them that I'm encouraging cabbage white butterfies and moths; into the garden, but there's a good reason; they are food for so many other animals, from bats to hedgehogs. Butterflies are a part of the natural food chain and the decline in the butterfly population is likely to have an impact on other species.

Providing a healthy environment for as wide a range of wildlife as possible has been and continues to be important to us. By offering a range of habitat we hope to increase biodiversity, which will help us as pests arrive in the garden. Over the next few years I hope to see a balance in the pest/predator ratio in the garden.

There is another type of pest that is truly unwelcome, but appears almost wherever poultry are kept. Rats are a nuisance and potentially deadly for poultry; a hungry rat will, given the opportunity, break into poultry housing and take young birds.

Not very long after we moved here, I stood at the kitchen sink gazing out of the window and watched four voles playing in the shelter of the stable. They were scampering around and tumbling over each other. I smiled to myself at the sight of these creatures playing so happily, unaware that they were being watched. It turned out that they weren't voles at all; they were young rats and, no doubt, were delighted to have a new supply of chicken food to steal and gorge themselves on. Naivety is a wonderful thing! We dealt with them using an electric zapper contraption, which the manufacturers say is instant.

The neigbourhood cats also play their part in keeping the rodent population at bay. One in particular is an excellent catcher of all things mouse-shaped. He's a bruiser of a cat with beautiful dark, tabby markings and a gait that tells you he's in charge of his own destiny. He is one of the cats that regularly sings a duet with Monty in the small hours of the night, but during the day, Monty is happy to watch him trot back and forth across our yard with his latest prize in his teeth.

Monty, too, has done his fair share of pest control, although I'm not entirely sure that he fully has the hang of it. He does like to show us what he's caught and so brings his catches into the house and proudly calls us to go and see what he has. Unfortunately, he hasn't quite learnt how to call us with clenched teeth, so invariably the 'caught thing' rapidly becomes 'uncaught'.

The first time he brought a rat into the kitchen I was a little surprised to see that it was still very much alive. What happened next seemed to be in slow motion. As he proudly meowed at us, the rat fell from his mouth; it seems as though its legs were already making a running movement before its feet hit the kitchen floor and within a blink, it had scuttled under the kitchen island unit.

It's not one of those fancy built in island units; we put it there not very long after we moved in. I didn't have enough storage space for all the cooking pans, mixing bowls and casserole dishes, so Mr J kindly created a wooden base upon which we put two double cupboards acquired via Freecycle.

It seemed that the gap below the cupboards was the perfect size for a rat to hide in; Monty looked confused, and having not seen the rat disappear under the cupboards, he looked at us accusingly. He seemed less than impressed that his lovely catch had disappeared, so he turned around and headed back outside, leaving us in the kitchen, open mouthed and ever-so-slightly horrified at the new resident in our kitchen.

We shouldn't have doubted Monty's catching abilities; early the next morning, the offending animal had been caught and left on the floor for me to trip over.

Nowadays we have got used to hearing that particular call that Monty makes and rush to see what he has brought in, with the hope that, before he lets whatever it is go, we can encourage him to take it back outside.

Monty

COLLECTING WATER

The site is around 150 feet (50m) above sea level. It slopes very slightly and gently, being only 5 feet higher on one side than the other and water flows from west to east towards the River Severn. There are no natural water sources on the site, no spring or stream, but it does have plenty of outbuildings which means that I could potentially catch rainwater.

Much of the guttering around the outbuildings is missing, but there's good guttering on the small conservatory at the back of the house, on the stable roof and on the large woodstore that had become the chicken palace. There was one water butt to capture rainwater from the chicken palace roof, but the other roofs had no systems in place to save this precious resource. I found a couple of water butts being given away on Freecycle and added one to the existing system,;the smaller water butt I used in the garden to make liquid fertiliser.

For the gutter on the conservatory we bought a pre-used IBC container which had previously contained food stuff. We raised it up on old concrete blocks and a pallet and Mr J re-routed the water from the downpipe by creating a rather Heath Robinson-style set of pipe-work to deliver the captured rainwater.

Between the two areas, we have almost 1500 litres of water stored at any one time, which I add to by having a couple of large dustbins in the garden which I transfer rainwater to in buckets and watering cans, whenever I remember.

Most years, for much of the year, there is adequate rainfall to keep the plants growing happily, but for a few weeks in late spring and early summer when the seedlings are small, I have used the water from the butts and dustbins to supplement the rainfall. And, if all else fails, I use a hosepipe.

We looked at the possibility of fitting slimline water butts to the wall outside the bathrooms to feed into the toilet cisterns; but as yet we still haven't had them fitted. It's on our very long list of things to do.

Given the gentleness of the slope across the site and how difficult it is to dig into the ground, I decided not to create swales and berms to slow down the flow of water and instead looked at which types of plants I was putting in each area, with the moisture loving plants in the lower areas of the paddock and those which prefer a Mediterranean climate at the higher, drier points. For the most part, this has worked well enough with a few exceptions when I planted before thinking it through. There is a rhubarb, Timperley Early, which could do with moving to a place where the rain water puddles as it wilts in its current position from the heat of the sun and the water draining away from it all too quickly.

Rhubarb Timperley Early is harvested
from late winter to late July

I've created two small ponds, one for the ducks and one to attract
wildlife. Both were made by laying logs onto the ground and covering
them with old butyl liner; they are crude affairs, but are effective, so I
haven't yet been tempted to change them. I had hoped that the wildlife
pond would attract frogs and toads, but I haven't seen any spawn in the
pond. There are some toads in the garden, but they are usually well-
hidden because of the chickens and ducks and I rarely find them as I'm
pottering outside. I spotted one caught by a chicken; sadly it didn't last
very long once a flock of inquisitive chickens had found it. The wildlife
pond has been home to many dragonflies and damselflies, waterboat-
men and other common aquatic creatures. Birds use it to drink from
and bees are seen perching on the marginal plants to take tiny sips from
the pond too. Nothing much seems to survive in the ducks' pond and I've
noticed that they 'tidy up' the wildlife pond when they have access to it
during the cooler months; this may be why I have seen no frogspawn.

Dragonfly visiting a honeysuckle flower

The wildlife pond

BUILDING ON MISTAKES

My construction skills are, at best, dubious, but I'm always eager to have a go and see what I can put together. As I still wasn't back to full health, many of the projects that I wanted to build were completely out of the question, but other, smaller projects could be tackled and I started experimenting with creating box-shaped frames to cover with chicken wire that became runs for the chickens and also ducklings.

Despite liking lists, I really don't like drawing out plans for building things. Until very recently I would much rather have held some pieces of wood together and seen what it would look like and then made it up as I went along. I don't recommend this approach; it can be costly in terms of wasted wood and other resources and it can also be very frustrating.

More recently I have started to draw rough sketches of projects I want to tackle, so that I have a clearer understanding of the processes, tools and materials that will be needed. This feels like a major step forward because it is a sign that I am starting to have faith in my understanding of how things are constructed and my ability to put them together without the endless trial and error stages of past projects.

At the end of 2016, we had hurriedly cobbled together a covered run to bridge the space between the shed that the chickens slept in and the stable where they were to spend their days. An enforced enclosure of the birds was announced due to a particularly virulent strain of avian influenza. We bought lengths of roof battening which is treated with an almost flamingo pink preservative. We cut the long lengths and Mr J knocked them into the ground to form the upright supports and we created cross braces and roof braces.

I then covered it in chicken wire and debris netting. Keeping the birds in the enclosed space was a protective measure, albeit a legally required one, and after just a couple of weeks we realised that we needed a more substantial roof on the covered walkway. In the piggeries I found some discarded sheets of twin wall polycarbonate and I also ordered some sheets of plywood from the local builders' merchant. Alternating the clear and plywood sheets on the roof of the walkway gave the chickens a light and airy outside area that would be safe for them to be in. In hindsight I wish that we had made it about four inches taller, so that Mr J didn't need to duck down when he walked through it. We were using the lengths of wood as economically as possible, so we cut them in half and that was the height of the walkway.

Following that I made mobile chicken runs and small enclosed mobile pens so that the ducklings could safely experience sunshine and

Covered walkway for the chickens to move between their shed and the stable/chicken condo

grass and gates. A second covered area for the second flock of chickens that slept in the chicken palace and then a walk-in brassica cage.

I still wouldn't describe my DIY carpentry skills as very good, but they are sufficiently adequate to be able to create some rudimentary structures and that's enough to get by with for the foreseeable future.

The shallow raised beds in the vegetable garden were a great place to start growing vegetables, but for better root crops I wanted to have deeper raised beds because carrots and parsnips were growing well enough, but once they reached the level of the soil in the paddock, they were bending and forking around its heavy clay and stones. A few parsnips that grew in the paddock soil, where I had dropped seeds or where they had self-sown, had grown to be huge roots. They were enormous parsnips, but incredibly difficult to get out of the ground.

It would have been lovely to have been able to build and fill beds that were 2 feet or more high, saving my knees and back from working so hard as I bent and knelt down to work, but we had neither the wood for the raised beds nor the soil and compost to fill them.

Not wanting to be beaten by a lack of resources, I had a look around to see if there was anything that I could use to make at least one raised bed a bit deeper. As luck would have it, we had an old wardrobe that we had brought with us from Mr J's mother's home. It was past its best, to say the least, and was quietly starting to fall apart. Mr J dismantled it and I used the larger pieces of wood for a variety of tasks like the slide-out front for a compost heap and a ramp for the chickens to access their coop.

Parsnips grown in the soil of the field were large, but very hard to harvest

Extending the depth of a raised bed with recycled wood

Using what we have on site has been key to keeping costs down – including drawer fronts

The drawer sides were cut into lengths and inserted vertically around the edges of a raised bed and the drawer fronts were also used. It wasn't pretty, but it was effective enough to allow me to fill a bed with additional compost and grow some really nice parsnips.

After creating the drawer-front raised bed, I looked for more visually appealing ways and something that was less work intensive to raise the levels of the beds and spotted online that some people use pallet collars. Having found a great source for pallets, I asked them if they had any pallet collars that we could buy and little by little we have acquired plenty of them. I've also used some of the long lengths of wood from dismantled pallets. With practice I have become more accurate and able to make raised beds look less thrown together and more uniform. When we took delivery of some 15-feet-long pallets, making deep raised beds became a real possibility and we started by creating a deep bed for asparagus.

COMPLETING THE RAISED BEDS

Over the course of the second year I finished making the beds in the annual vegetable garden using more pallet collars and individual lengths of wood taken from pallets.

Pallet collars are simply constructed: four lengths of wood that are hinged on the corners and can be stacked. I cut one of the longer sides of each pallet collar and opened it out to make a long U shape which I could place to create a raised bed. Another opened pallet collar at the other end of the bed gave a framework and I used lengths of wood taken from pallets to join the two collars together.

Two of the beds still don't have a frame around them and I now plant directly into the ground with its clay soil and, if I find some suitable wood, I will make edges for those beds.

The plants don't care what the framework looks like, the wildlife doesn't care about appearances and if I'm working with nature, with its rhythms and patterns, then I feel I should worry less about aesthetics and more about building the soil and microbial life in it.

Soil and its living organisms are a fascinating and complex subject, which I've been learning more about over the last few years; I feel as though as much as I learn, I find that there is even more to find out. And this ever-expanding potential for learning is one of the things that draws me to homesteading and, especially, to gardening.

> No matter how eager I am for the garden to look neat and co-ordinated, it takes time to develop a new garden on a tight budget and rushing just isn't necessary.

RECORDING OUR PROGRESS

I use my phone to make notes, so I don't have to take pen and paper into the garden and then struggle to read my scribbly writing when I get back indoors. I dictate my thoughts as I walk around the garden and listen back to them and make notes when I have time. I find this much more effective and more detailed as I can listen to my running commentary of thoughts about a particular raised bed, plant or idea, as long as I start my recording with the date for reference. I also try to remember to state what the weather is like that day, so that I have a reasonable record of how wet or dry, hot or cold the growing season has been.

I had started writing a blog at the time that we put in the offer to purchase our smallholding and had used it as a way to keep a record of the changes and progression of the transition from paddock to gardens as well as recording the changes to our health and wellbeing. As I became more and more immersed in life here, I found writing a blog too restricting and increasingly difficult to explain in detail, the things that I was doing on a day to day basis.

BLOG

I've been very quiet on the blogging front for the last couple of weeks because so much has been going on here and I've been somewhat reactive rather than pro-active. Last month I went to my GP for a standard blood test as required every few weeks or months to check that my thyroid medication is at the correct level. The GP said that she was concerned that my need for an increase in medication combined with a couple of other symptoms that we had discussed, may actually be masking something more sinister. She then went on to tell me that she wanted to test for uterine and ovarian cancer, heart disease, kidney malfunction and lung cancer. Well, talk about pulling the rug out from under somebody's feet, I was horrified and terrified at the same time. I'm sure she said lots of 'don't panic' type phrases, but if she did, I didn't hear them.

All I could think about was that my father had suffered and eventually died from heart disease and my mother liver and spleen cancer which had travelled to her lungs. Having cared for my mother (with my sister) through those last few weeks, the memories of the, quite frankly, hideous death that she had, came flooding back. All the images that I had locked away were now swimming around my brain.

So I went for an ultrasound scan, a chest x-ray, a raft of blood and urine tests, an ECG and more blood tests. I was called back in for additional blood tests, twice! For almost a month I was walking around wondering whether my body's autoimmune disease had finally turned on other parts of my insides.

Until the GP raised all these potential issues I had felt fine, absolutely marvellous actually and now I was wondering if my slight shortness of breath wasn't just due to being overweight, but was it a symptom of one of the conditions that the GP was looking for? Every niggle became a nag and a worry.

Now I know that it is pointless in worrying before the event, but our minds play tricks on us and I was losing sleep, losing a lot of sleep, worrying that I was harbouring a silent killer. Yes I know it all sounds ridiculously dramatic, but when you are staring at the ceiling at three in the morning yet again, everything becomes somewhat out of perspective.

Life on the smallholding continued as much as possible as normal; I kept as calm as I could on the surface and cracked on with the jobs that needed doing and making plans for the garden, the poultry and the house. Mr J had to rearrange a couple of work days so that he could take me to appointments, but otherwise things seemed normal. The chicks were growing well, the chickens were happy, we took delivery of some new chickens, life carried on as it should.

But in my head it was a very different matter, I have been in a state of panic for a month and inevitably that takes its toll on the body and on one's mood and I am sure that I have been pretty difficult to live with over the last month. Thank goodness Mr J is so understanding!

Finally on Wednesday this week, a full month since the previous appointment that started this chain of events, I returned to the GP to hear the results of all the tests. It seems I am not harbouring anything unpleasant and there appears little to worry about.

There is an anomaly on my ECG and given my father's health history, she is referring my results to a cardiologist to check whether any other action should be taken, but I'm not really worried about that. When I was having the ECG done I was half sitting, half lying on the most uncomfortable couch so I'm not surprised that it was showing as having a minor blip; I was in pain and not really relaxing as required. And, she is referring my ultrasound results to a gynaecologist just to check that there are no issues there, but she couldn't see anything untoward.

I can only tell you that this has been a very difficult month. I have felt very alone and very frightened. I have also taken stock of my life and am really rather happy with how I'm living and what I'm doing.

I decided that if I had either heart disease or cancer of some kind that I would enjoy each day, live life to the full, celebrate the new morning, be grateful and thankful for all my blessings. And, if I didn't have a health issue, I would do the same, but also celebrate my good health each and every day. It has taken a few days for my brain to readjust, to stop panicking and to start this celebratory routine. Last night, for the first time in quite a while I slept for seven hours non-stop and have woken up feeling refreshed and ready to start this next chapter.

So here's to good health, to a loving family, to a bright future!

Excerpt from 17th April 2017

A special gift on my birthday changed the way I created videos

Watching videos on YouTube, I became convinced that recording our progress in video format was the way forward. Not only would I be able to show in detail the projects and progress, but there was a potential for a small income from making the videos. In mid-January 2017, I published the first of what was to become a daily vlog about life on our smallholding on my YouTube channel Liz Zorab – Byther Farm. I used my mobile phone to record videos and edited them on the free software on my computer. They were not masterpieces of cinematic art. I felt awkward and gawky, fumbled over my words and it took me a while to get used to not looking at the screen on my phone and to talk looking at the lens.

A year later Mr J gave me a camera for my birthday and I purchased editing software and, for a total of 19 months, I created an almost-daily video. It was, without a doubt, exhausting, but it was a new creative outlet and, on many days, was good fun too. I no longer make purely vlog-style videos; instead I offer instructional and, hopefully, inspirational videos and produce just one or two videos per week, but I continue to record the progress and development of the site on film and carefully catalogue it to ensure that I have it to use as a reference for the future.

Although I have chosen to publicly share some aspects of our life on this smallholding, we are, undoubtedly, very private people. There is no great desire to be recognised in the street or to have people arrive for a visit unannounced or uninvited, so we decided to give the channel a name that gave it an identity without compromising our privacy.

We had many lively and silly conversations about potential names for the farm; we translated names into Welsh using 'Google translate' and fell about laughing at the number of times we just couldn't pronounce the words correctly. We wanted a name that meant something to us, but at the same time meant nothing at all.

One evening, after a glass or two of a particularly nice elderberry wine, Mr J started talking about where our home is located. It's by the road, by the river, by the village, by the bridge, by the farm. Boom! There it was: an accurate description of where we lived. I was slightly worried that people would pronounce it as one word – bythe – rather than two words, so I suggested that we added an R on to the end of it. This would also give a nice Bristolian pronunciation to it, as a nod to the city that had been my home for so long. The local Bristol accent has a West Country sound, with many words pronounced as though they either have an R or L at the end of them, even when there isn't one.

Secure in the knowledge that we had made up this word and therefore it was bound to be unique, I added the phrase Byther Farm to my name for the channel title. Well how wrong were we! Over the last three years, I have been contacted on more than one occasion by some lovely people with the surname Byther, asking if we were any relation to them. And there's a blues musician called Byther Smith too. So much for our moment of genius!

50 DAYS OF HARVEST

In early summer 2017 I set myself a challenge of harvesting 5lbs (2.2kg), in weight, of food a day for 50 days. Each day I harvested, weighed and recorded the different fruit and vegetables that were ready for harvesting. I quietly hoped that I would harvest more than 250lbs (113kg), but if not, it would still be a great start to filling our freezers and cupboards for the year.

By the start of the second week, it became apparent that the target was too low and that I should increase it, so I doubled it to 500 pounds of food in 50 days. I didn't include anything that was picked and eaten in the garden and only included food that was prepared and stored away that day.

In hindsight, it was a really good exercise in disciplining myself to ensure that I had cleaned, chopped, blanched or whatever was needed to put the food into storage before harvesting the next batch of food.

Over the 50-day period of summer and early autumn, I harvested, picked and foraged over 800lbs (363kg) of food and was delighted to have surpassed my own expectations.

The video thumbnail introducing the 50 Days of Harvest series

LIST OF HARVEST FROM 50 DAYS OF HARVEST

317lbs (144kg) apples (305lbs (138kg) windfalls, 12lbs (6kg) from our own trees)

85lbs (39kg) winter squash

22lbs (10kg) beetroot

30lbs (14kg) dwarf French beans

44lbs (22kg) courgette (zucchini)

57lbs (26kg) tomatoes

3lbs (1kg) cucumbers

1lb (0.5kg) parsnips

9lbs (4kg) plums

48lbs (22kg) runner beans

8lbs (4kg) savoy cabbage

31lbs (14kg) Borlotti beans

9lbs (4kg) blackberries

31lbs (14kg) pears

16lbs (7kg) raspberries

19lbs (9kg) sweetcorn

3lbs (1kg) Greek gigantes beans

75lbs (34kg) chicken and duck

plus as many eggs as we wanted each week

This list didn't include food harvested before or after those 50 days, but gives a good indication of the kinds of foods I was storing away.

By the end of our second year here I knew that, all things being equal, the garden could provide us with enough food to eat well for a whole year.

It was a strange feeling to acknowledge that I had managed to grow sufficient food for us, that I had done what I set out to do in terms of providing our food, in just two years. There are still foodstuffs that we buy at the supermarket because we like them (tea, coffee, dairy products) or because we choose to eat them out of season (melons) and we still buy toiletries, but over all our food bill has plummeted and the quality of the food that we eat has soared.

During our end of year assessment of how well or not the season had gone and the setting of goals for the next year, we were excited by the potential for growing more food. The soil in the raised beds was not as healthy as it could be and as it improved, so would the likelihood of more abundant harvests. We hadn't yet started expanding the growing areas across the rest of the site and food forest was still in its very early stages. We both started to envisage the possibilities and what might come in future years.

Our goals for 2018 included:

- More of the same, but different.
- Have a more planned programme of hatching chicks and ducklings.
- Some of the fence posts around the perimeter needed replacing as they had rotted at ground level.
- Exploring the idea of keeping sheep in the paddock not yet turned into vegetable garden.
- Build a veranda or sundeck next to the house.
- Build a wooden pergola or tunnel in the garden to grow climbers like grapevines.
- Improve my winemaking skills.
- Tidy the inside of the barn (this goal has been rolled forward each year; the barn almost sighs at me each time I go into it).

On gusty days, the wind is a little hair-raising

WORKING ON A WINDY SITE

I don't recall it being windy on the days that we viewed our home before we purchased it. Perhaps it was windy and I was just so spellbound by the views and the potential that I didn't notice, but we certainly knew about the wind by the time Mr J had moved all of our possessions into the house.

As part of designing the gardens in the paddock, I created a series of rooms. Each room or area is now bordered by fences or hedges, or both, to help slow down the passage of the wind across the site and to give some protection to the plants growing in it. The hedge on the west boundary, which still hasn't grown tall enough to provide any real windbreak will, I hope, eventually be the first line of defence. The fence surrounding the vegetable garden will have fruit hedging on the west side of the garden and compost bays on the east. Trees and shrubs slow the wind's journey in the Patrons' Garden and the hedge on the east boundary is now filling out nicely to form a good shelter when the cold easterlies arrive in the autumn and winter.

While I was waiting for the hedges to grow enough to provide an effective windbreak, I looked at other ways to reduce the impact of the wind. As I have replaced or refreshed raised beds, they have been made taller, the soil remaining at the same level as before but the deeper sides of the beds provide a little shelter.

Single bamboo canes in the ground for climbers have been replaced by more elaborate, sturdier structures and I've looked for shorter growing varieties of some plants e.g. dwarf French beans thrive while their taller cousins can struggle in the breeze.

After three years of trial and error, but mostly error, I decided that the runner bean structure that I've used in the past just wasn't strong enough to cope with the winds that have arrived each August. Each year, I made the bean support a little sturdier, but once heavily laden with bean plants, the wind has caught them, snapping the bamboo canes, and unceremoniously dumped them on the ground.

Using what we had on site, Mr J pounded some 5 feet (150cm) long chestnut posts into the ground at the corners and midpoint of the runner bean bed. I screwed lengths of pallet wood to them as near to the top as I could and then fixed the bamboo canes to the horizontal pieces of wood with cable ties. It looks like the type of thing to which a cowboy would have fastened his horse while he went into the saloon! This support structure has now been

tested during two years of weather and the beans have stayed upright and off the floor.

I put the canes into the ground, not in the usual A frame shape, but more like an inverted A. Like this the beans hang down over the pathway and are more easily accessible than they would be if all the growth was bunched close together at the apex of a more traditional A frame bean support.

No single wind-breaking measure has been successful on its own, but the combination of windbreak fabrics, more mature plants, higher sided raised beds and hedging are starting to reduce the impact of the wind little by little.

The two most positive, if unplanned, results of creating a series of rooms are that no one garden space feels too big to cope with tending, and that hedges, edges and boundaries are highly fertile and active offering a mixture of habitat for wildlife and plants. The compost bay fence on the east side of the vegetable garden provides homes for untold numbers of insects, worms and small animals and nest materials for birds. I use the heat and nutrients of the composting materials to encourage plants to grow by planting squashes in them and eventually the compost, with its microbial life, is put back onto the growing spaces.

of £199.50

We built a sturdy bean
support frame from
materials we had on site

Colourful borlotti beans

Overhead view with room
boundaries marked

MAKING THE MOST OF MISTAKES

I have made so many mistakes while we've been here and, hopefully, I have learnt something as a result of each one. Sometimes those lessons have been of a practical nature of how not to do something; other times I have learnt something about me as a person, my outlook or my attitude.

Mistakes range from:

- ▸ Planting dwarf (bush) beans only to discover that I hadn't labelled the envelope of saved seeds correctly and they were climbing beans.
- ▸ Not watering seedlings enough.
- ▸ Hoeing away rows of vegetable seedlings.
- ▸ Forgetting to sow enough/any of a particular type of vegetable.
- ▸ Not making fences robust enough to exclude poultry from the vegetable garden.
- ▸ Trusting turkeys not to fly up onto the barn roof and decline to come back down.
- ▸ Planting too close together when the eventual size of a shrub will be much too large for the allotted space.
- ▸ Not keeping on top of the weeding in areas that need to be kept clear.
- ▸ Letting thistles go to seed.

And the list goes on and on.

The biggest change that I have noticed is how I deal with mistakes. Where I used to get upset, feel disappointed or frustrated and then get cross with myself for the errors, I am now much more relaxed and spend time thinking about what I've learnt and try to make sure that I can remember the lessons learnt for next time. It is a gentler way to treat myself and the process of growing food.

A BREATH OF FRESH AIR

In August we were paid a visit by Tony and Louise, friends made online via Mr J's love of music. They are incredibly talented musicians who formed a band called Kafkadiva (and they also play in a successful Pink Floyd tribute group called Dark Side of the Wall). When I was first thinking about starting a YouTube channel, I wanted some music to have as a theme song and Mr J suggested a piece by Kafkadiva called Breathe; it was perfect! He contacted Louise and asked whether they would consider giving me permission to use the song. The response was delightful; not only were they happy for it to be used, they also sent me two different instrumental versions for use in the videos too. I love the words to the chorus, 'I know we can do it, I'm sure we can do it, we've just got to breathe' and I have used this piece of music in almost every video since I published the first (then daily) vlog in January 2017.

Sometimes when you get to know someone from a distance, meeting them face to face can be awkward and they don't match up to the personality you have visualised in your head. Tony and Louise turned out to be as nice as, if not nicer, than we had imagined and their time with us flew past. We had a lovely evening filled with food and drink, laughter and more laughter and I was rather sad that they had to leave so soon. But they did promise to return after the winter and they did just that.

Seeing them again was like family coming home after a long spell away. There was much hugging and smiles, and news to catch up with over a long evening meal and another steady flow of laughter. They timed their visit to coincide with the release of the second Kafkadiva album, *Dysfunctionormal*. For the second time in a year, songs were performed in the kitchen; not only was it great to listen to their new songs, but it was wonderful to see Mr J so happy to have live music around him. Both Tony and Mr J are drummers and I'm sure Mr J won't mind me saying that he is a little rustier in his skills than Tony. Louise and I left them to talk all things drums and music and we headed out into the garden to talk about plants and wildlife.

Both of these gentle friends are knowledgeable about birds; it was lovely that they spotted and named the birds that I had seen living in or visiting our garden, but couldn't identify. Once again, their visit felt too short; I would have been happy for them to stay with us for a week rather than just the weekend, but work duties called and they needed to return home.

After they had gone, we reflected on our good fortune; we have been very lucky to make friends with some wonderful people over the last few years. Refreshed after a weekend of not-the-norm activities, I felt ready to return to work in the garden with a renewed vigour in my step.

DUCKS IN THE FOOD FOREST

Another surprisingly calming influence is the ducks, especially when they are free to roam in the food forest. We both take so much pleasure in hearing their gentle noises and their relatively slow movements. Apart from their ability to hunt out and eat slugs and snails, the ducks provide humour and a sense of completeness to the garden that I can't quite put into words.

The ducks were allowed to forage in the food forest for much of the year. They have a passion for currants and berries and ate quite a lot of our harvest before I realised that they had done so.

A lesson for future years was that they needed to be excluded from the area while the currants and berries were forming and ripening.

Ducks show little respect for manmade boundaries. Raised beds are just an inconvenience, but are not insurmountable and indeed, they quickly learn to hop up into a raised bed, squash many of the plants and uproot others. Free roaming ducks are not for the faint-hearted, but if you can forgive them their messiness and their stomping feet, they are a delight to have as companion gardeners.

White Lady
runner beans
ready to dry for
storage

HARVESTING AND STORING – DRYING

During our first couple of years here, I used freezing as the main method for storing food, but I also explored the possibilities of drying more of our food. I popped beans out of their pods and spread them out on trays to dry and once they were completely dry, I stored them in jars. I invested in a low-mid range priced dehydrator, persuaded by others that dehydrating food was a great way to store it. I dried some herbs successfully; I have used those well and have continued to dry some herbs like marjoram, oregano and thyme. As for drying fruit or vegetables, sadly all I could think of was the dried Vesta meals of my childhood, when humankind was racing to the moon and all things space-related were in vogue. The meals came in sachets, the contents of which were added to water and then cooked until the dried ingredients were soft and ready to eat. As a child I disliked the consistency of the rehydrated vegetables and that dislike remains today, except maybe for some beans, pulses and other foods like pasta. The only dried fruit that I'm terribly keen on is vine fruits and plums (prunes).

The other off-putting thing about dehydrating food was the noise of the dehydrator. It may be that the particular model I chose was a noisy one. It sounded like a hairdryer, which going for days at a time to dry foods was just too noisy for our liking. Our kitchen is a quiet place; there is one small built-in refrigerator and the low hum that it makes is muffled by being inside the kitchen units. Having the hairdryer sound echoing around the kitchen was, at best, irritating.

There is great value in knowing yourself as a cook and by the time I was harvesting beans in the third year, I still hadn't used the dried beans from year two. I just don't cook in an organised and planned way that allows me to know a day in advance that I'd like to use beans and put some in water to rehydrate to use them in cooking. I did however use some of them as seeds for the next year and I gave some to friends, so they weren't wasted.

beet leaves   parsnips
rhubarb   asparagus   chard
leeks   beetroots
spinach   parsley   mint
chives   garlic as perennials
strawberries   lettuce
broad (fava) bean tips   onions
walking onions   globe artichoke
lemon balm   red orach
Asturian tree cabbage
elderflower   raspberries
white currants
blackberries   redcurrants
blackcurrants   tayberries
loganberries
potatoes   peas   red cabbage
lovage   turnips
calendula   dill   herb fennel
radish   nasturtiums
courgette (zucchini)   cucumbers

YEAR THREE

2018

GROW A GIFT

CELEBRATING ABUNDANCE

Starting the year with the freezers and store cupboards filled with food and with winter crops in the ground gave us an enormous sense of security. Knowing that we would be able to eat a varied diet of home-grown, tasty fruit and vegetables took away the worry and pressure of being the food provider and allowed me to concentrate on resting and recovering from the physical exertion of the hectic harvesting period and the mental drudgery of getting through the darker months.

After years of cooking meals for growing children, I still haven't learnt to cook for just the two of us which means that on many days there is a surplus of cooked food that can be portioned into containers and frozen for use at a later date. I also purposefully batch cook to have ready meals in the freezer.

As I wind down in the early winter, Mr J starts the busiest period at his job off site and having pre-made home cooked meals in the freezer that can be easily defrosted and heated has turned out to be a bit of a lifeline for us.

We have two freezers in the barn which are filled with basic ingredients harvested from the garden and foraged fruits. As I use the food from the freezers in the barn, I consolidate it from the two freezers into one, to make it run more efficiently. In theory, eventually both freezers in the barn could be switched off until the next harvest is gathered. It hasn't quite worked like that, but I have switched off one of the freezers each year after we have eaten enough food that there was only sufficient stored to fill one freezer. In the house, there is one large and one small freezer which, for the most part, are filled with pre-cooked meals, pre-portioned vegetables, fruit, sauces and stock giving us a good range and choice of meals readily at hand.

A tall cupboard in the kitchen acts as a simple pantry for homemade preserves and chutneys. I thought that during the previous autumn I had made sufficient jams, jellies (jam without the bits), chutneys and sauces to last throughout the year, but inevitably some things were more popular than others and to this day there are still a couple of jars of green tomato chutney, labelled 2017, lurking at the back of one of the shelves. Perhaps that speaks more of my management of stock rotation than our eating preferences.

Batch cooked meals ready for the freezer

Homemade jams, jellies and other preserves are stored in the pantry cupboard

Nowadays fifty-three really isn't any age at all. It wouldn't be unusual for there to be at least thirty years ahead of me and yet I remember women of the same age when I was a child seeming old. Often with stout ankles, large tummies and bosom and grey permed hair. Sturdy women. So what's changed? Well, plenty! The beauty industry, media industry and health-care services all have a part to play and I am pleased about some of it (although not the media images that we have to compete with in our heads each day!). I have also come to understand that perhaps many, many women (and some men too) were suffering with undiagnosed or untreated thyroid issues. My conjecture is based not on scientific or factual evidence but on my own sturdy experience and is, therefore, highly subjective and of course, just my own sturdy opinion.

I was going to write about this today and explain in depth about why and how rotten I feel most of the time, about how chronic illness has not only affected me but my family, partner and friendships, but now I've changed my mind and will write about other things instead. After all, why would I inflict my low or pain-filled days upon you? You may be having a really good day and just read it with interest (or disinterest), but you may feel low and quite frankly, there's enough feeling low without my ha'penny worth adding to it. Now before I upset anyone, I am not saying that we shouldn't share our stories and I really do understand why folks share their situations online and often admire them for being so forthright and honest in their writings and how some folk can share their stories without getting into 'woe is me' mode. Sometimes by sharing our stories, a huge amount of good is achieved; people's attitudes are changed and massive amounts of money can be raised for charities that support others with illnesses. I may well share my story one day, but not today. I do keep an online diary of how I am and how I am feeling, but it's kept within a closed community of people who are dealing with the same health issues and where we can offer support to each other.

I'm conscious that sometimes when I write my blog, it can appear that my life is all roses and no thorns, all sunny (even when it rains) and almost too good to be true. It's not, I have the same frustrations, worries and difficulties as everyone else, I just choose not to focus on them too much when writing my blog. Over the last three years Mr J and I have been faced with some of those big life moments that are highly stressful and we have grown together and stronger not because of them, but because of the way in which we have chosen to deal with them. Along the way we have both sat with our mothers as they were dying and had to deal with being executors, clearing parents' homes of 30+ years of belongings and memories and selling their homes, when all the while we were still grieving. Between us we've coped with moving in together, being made redundant, having very stress-filled jobs, moving house again and being rather poorly. Through all of these changes we have shared the constant security of each other's love, respect and support. And we have humour!

Excerpt from 7th March 2016

LIVING THE DREAM?

People often say to us that we are living the dream and it could be easy to become complacent about how we live, but I am constantly mindful that we are incredibly fortunate and privileged.

To maintain this lifestyle, we have made some major changes to how we live on a day to day basis; some of those changes were forced upon us by circumstances, others were a matter of choice.

❖ Not long before we moved here, I had stopped driving because I didn't feel safe behind the steering wheel; my vision and hearing were declining rapidly as was my spatial awareness, but more than anything I simply struggled to stay awake for very long and falling asleep whilst driving was just not something I was prepared to risk happening.

In the depths of being ill, I didn't just doze off gently, I completely zonked out, often mid-sentence; it must have been so frustrating for Mr J. We used to have a television in the bedroom, so that I had some entertainment while I lay in bed waiting for my thyroid and the rest of my body to respond to the medication and supplements. Mr J bought box sets of television dramas for me to watch. Episode after episode, I would fall asleep within a short time of it starting, so had absolutely no idea about the story unfolding on the screen. When we rewatched them at a later date, they suddenly made so much more sense.

There was no point in continuing to pay for the upkeep and insurance of a car that wasn't going to be driven, so we made the decision that I would sell my car and we'd become a one car family. This felt like a big deal; it felt like I had surrendered my independence and, having driven myself everywhere I needed (and wanted) to go since I was 17 years old, I was suddenly relying on Mr J to take me to appointments, shopping or even to social events. The reality was that I was just too unwell to go on social outings; I couldn't walk around the local food store without using the trolley to lean on or without struggling to pick things up whilst also using a walking stick and I also needed to stop and rest every few minutes, and so the only time I left our home was for the regular doctor and hospital appointments.

It wasn't until the middle of 2018 that I felt well enough and safe to drive again, but I disliked driving the little van that we had bought. Well that's not entirely true. I couldn't get the van out of first gear; I just couldn't manipulate the gear stick in the way it needed to be done to drive at anything over 5mph!

Now that we have a different vehicle, one that I can comfortably drive, we still choose to be a one car family because it makes sense financially and also it reduces our environmental impact. I am sure that the time will come when we may have to look again at having a second car, but it's not a decision that we will make lightly and we would, mostly likely, opt for an electric or hydrogen powered car.

❖ Mr J is supplied with a uniform for his work and as I am based at home, we no longer need to buy smart clothes for work as we did in our previous roles. Most of the clothes that we buy now are purchased from thrift stores or charity shops with the exception of underwear and shoes, because no one wants ill-fitting undies or pinched toes.

❖ There are other purchases that we no longer make, now that we work at or close to home; things like food on the go, coffee shop drinks and snacks, lunches in cafés or restaurants have all disappeared from our lives.

As a result of my change of diet to gluten free foods (to help support my digestive system) and because of a raft of allergies and sensitivities to food, we no longer go out to eat. Sometimes I miss it; I miss artisanal pizzas from our local pub, a warm three cheese quiche from a farm shop café and even the greasy sweet and sour meals that we bought at the local take-away. More than the food itself, I miss the process of going out to eat, the sociability and the cementing of friend-ships over a cup of tea and slice of cake. What I don't miss is spending all that money on food that ultimately was simply adding more and more weight to my body. Looking back, I am shocked at the amount of money we used to spend on tea, coffee and snacks. It's a significant saving that we continue to make on a daily basis.

My favourite square in Gamla Stan, Stockholm, home to the Nobel Museum

❖ We don't take holidays.

Choosing to tighten our belts, in terms of day to day spending, is one thing; choosing a lifestyle that means you may not be able to go away overnight is another and it's a choice that we made almost without thinking about it.

During our last two or three holidays abroad, I had struggled with the flights, struggled with walking around the cities that we were visiting. I was exhausted for most of the time we were away and then for days or even weeks once we had returned home. We didn't know that my thyroid was malfunctioning, we didn't know about Hashimoto's thyroid-itis and we didn't know that much of our lifestyle was making it worse.

Returning from our last trip to Stockholm to see Mr J's family, I realised that it was likely to be the last trip that I was to make abroad as I found travelling just too hard on my body. After we had settled into life on Byther Farm and my mobility had improved, we thought about getting away for a few nights to see friends in other parts of the UK, but the logistics were potentially a nightmare. I asked a couple of close friends whether they would be willing to be farm sitters. They were more than happy to come here to stay while we went away; four years later, we still haven't taken them up on the offer.

Mr J's annual leave from work is used as time to relax and unwind, to rest and recuperate and to tackle one larger project in the garden or house. I don't feel the need to have a holiday as such because I take great swathes of time each winter to rest and refresh and also because, more often than not, working in the garden and with the poultry is either so relaxing or so much fun that it feels like a holiday.

❧ We don't use a subscription-based or a pay per view television service. When those service providers first offered satellite and cable services, I didn't want them; I felt that as I already paid for a television licence, I didn't want to be paying even more to have the choice of yet more channels offering programmes that I didn't want to watch. I was delighted when I first learnt that Mr J felt the same way. We spend quite a lot of time creating videos and radio shows. Mr J has been producing at least one radio show per week for over 40 years (and he's got quite good at it) and I've been creating videos which are published on YouTube and Patreon since January 2017. Very often by the end of the day, the last thing either of us want is to watch yet another screen. When we read a book, it is of the paper variety.

❧ One of the biggest steps for our change in lifestyle was to become debt-free.

There is absolutely no way we could sustain this lifestyle if we were still servicing the debts of a mortgage, bank loans, car loans and credit cards that we had before we moved here.

We are not rich people in the monetary sense, but we are wealthy in many other ways that matter to us more. We decided that we value time at home and time together more than having additional cash in the bank and that going without a whole load of 'stuff' that we didn't really want anyway would be healthier for us in the long term. Mr J works off site part-time over four days per week and I work on site full time depending on the time of year.

The reed beds (left) are cleared on Valentine's Day (right)

We were able to buy our home outright because each of us had some funds from the sale of our previous homes and gifts left to us by our parents. We carefully chose a home that would have very few overheads and require very few regular payments as a way to minimise our outgoings.

The house has photovoltaic panels on the roof which generate electricity and by good fortune, the previous owners had installed them at a time when FIT (Feed-In Tariff) payments were at a very high rate and they had signed a 25-year contract which would be transferred to us when we bought the house. There are also solar panels on the other side of the roof which heat the water. In the winter it doesn't heat it very much in the weak winter sunshine, but it does warm the water a little which then reduces the amount of power used to heat the water to the desired temperature.

FIT payments were introduced in early 2010, by the UK government, to encourage householders to install 'green' energy sources. The scheme paid an amount of money to householders for each unit of electricity generated by renewable energy products, like photovoltaic panels and also an additional payment for any electricity that was not used in the house and was returned to the National Grid.

We were delighted to have a home that could generate a little income, which would help us pay for other energy costs (like heating fuel). I think that new FIT contracts may have now been stopped, which makes me even more grateful that the previous house owners joined the FIT scheme when they did.

Our waste water is dealt with on site too. Water from the bathrooms goes to a septic tank which then cleverly filters the liquid away to a reed bed system, where over the course of time the water works its way through the reeds and sandy soil to a settling pool and then away from the land in a soakaway. All gently done without the use of chemicals.

The reed beds require a little annual maintenance, but nothing so arduous that we can't do it ourselves. Once a year we clear away the dead reeds and tidy the area of weeds. The first year that we did this task, we enjoyed working on something in the garden together and then realised that it was Valentine's Day, so it has become our regular Valentine's Day activity.

CHANGES IN HEALTH

By early 2018, my GP informed me that the hormone levels in my thyroid had stabilised and I could remain on the same level of thyroid medication for the next year, and unless anything changed with how I felt, I did not need to return for the bi-monthly blood tests that I had undergone for the previous nearly three years; once a year would be the new testing schedule. I'm sure I should have been delighted with the news, but I was struggling with SAD and most of my emotions, as well as my energy levels, were subdued and flattened.

By spring, as my mood lifted, I was pleased not to be returning for the regular tests, not because they were unpleasant, but because it signalled that my body had found a new level of normality – and that had to be a good thing!

The myriad of vitamin and mineral supplements that I started taking when I first became ill had been adjusted, reduced and readjusted. It took a long time to work out which supplements were helping me to feel better and I did considerable research and reading before I took any of them.

As the garden produced a wider variety and greater volume of fresh fruit and vegetables, the need to supplement my diet with tablets reduced. As the thyroid medication started to work, I was absorbing more of the vitamins and minerals that I ate, further reducing the need for supplements. Nowadays, I take Vitamin D3 in line with NHS recommendations as well as a low dose of a Vitamin B complex and a few minerals. A bowl of mixed berries with some live culture yoghurt looks and tastes considerably more appetising than a handful of tablets and capsules.

I am convinced that the fresh air and exercise, the gentle rhythm of our lives and the unadulterated food that we eat all played their part in improving my health and continue to be the major contributing factors to our wellbeing.

MORE INTENTIONAL OBSERVATION

As the year began, I had resolved to be more observant; not just looking at what was around me, but actively seeing and noticing how things linked together. I started to record the patterns that I saw, the repetition of shapes right across the gravelled yard and the gardens. The regular morning frosts sat heavily on the ground, fences, plants, fixtures and fittings highlighting the patterns and shapes. As an observational exercise it was interesting, but more importantly it helped me to focus on objects and events outside myself and to make the intellectual and emotional links with nature that I find increasingly difficult as the winter goes on.

The semi-circular perfection of the frost highlighting the rings of the wood on the top of a fence post particularly caught my eye and I still spend time, every now and then, tracing the shapes on the fence posts with my fingers, feeling the roughness of the wood that insects now use as a home.

I have found it good practice to slow down and look with intention. In the spring and summer, this lets me see any new plants that I might like to keep, among the chaotic scramble of a patch of weeds. In the autumn I can more easily find the last few beans, rosehips or seeds that I want to harvest and save. In winter, I can see the patterns around us more clearly.

This intentional observation works well inside our home too. Taking time to look at the dynamics of our relationship, the little things that matter and the small actions that, in the long term, can mean so much and support each other's needs.

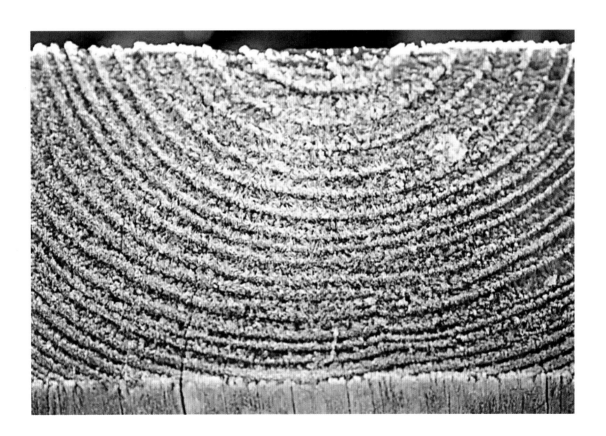

Snow at the front of the house

WANTING TO DO SOMETHING

Late winter had been harsh; the 'Beast from the East' enveloped the country in bitterly cold weather and deep snow that lingered. It kept us inside except for the times we needed to go outside to care for the poultry. Luckily for the birds, they come with built-in snuggly duvets that they permanently carry around with them. The chickens hunkered down in the old stable and barn and we made a makeshift additional shelter for the ducks that provided them with some protection from the bitter, almost spiteful, easterly winds.

As we struggled to keep warm with our wood burners lit and the central heating system pumping out heat 24 hours a day, I saw news reports of charities desperately trying to find shelter for homeless people; I couldn't imagine how frightened, cold and hungry they must have been. A seed of an idea was sown.

I wanted to be able to help in some way, to be able to offer something that might be of use to others. Time and time again my thoughts came back to those images I had seen of people, young and old, alone and huddled under layers of clothes and cardboard boxes in doorways, in a desperate attempt to keep warm enough to stay alive as the winter storms raged around them.

I knew I didn't feel up to opening up our home as a shelter, but I wanted to do something, to find some way that I could to express how I cared and how it matters that we don't leave our most vulnerable citizens to fend for themselves, particularly in such extreme weather conditions.

I decided to start small, to start with what I knew I could do; I could grow food. I would grow some extra plants: food that was grown with the intention of giving it away in the winter.

I was going to Grow A Gift.

This wasn't an entirely new activity. In December 2017, I made a food parcel donation via social services to a local family who would be struggling to provide a Christmas meal for themselves. I felt that it was important that this was done without fanfare or recognition; that was not why I wanted to make the donation. I just wanted to help in some small way and this was it. But I now wanted to do something more constructive, more organised and pre-planned.

In December 2018, I spotted a local community group that was providing meals on Christmas day for anyone who would be on their own for the day and I contacted them to offer the vegetables for the meal, as much as they needed to be able to provide each visitor with a traditional Christmas meal. I didn't have any carrots to give to them, but a few days before Christmas, a volunteer arrived to collect potatoes, parsnips, cabbages and leeks for the 30 people and volunteers expected.

In the spring of 2019, I once again sowed more seeds than I needed with the intention of donating some food to another local group providing meals, but this time I was ready to ask other gardeners to do the same. I made a video which I published on YouTube and invited viewers to take part in Grow A Gift 2019. The response was positive; other content creators made videos inviting their viewers to grow a gift and it seems that the idea was a popular one. It's an easy thing to do if you are already planting, for example, a few Brussels sprout plants; one more

won't be much extra work, but could potentially help to supply some warm food for someone who doesn't have access to it, at a time when it's really needed.

The basic concept was sound, and simple, but I had a lot of feedback towards the end of the year from gardeners saying that they couldn't find anywhere that would accept their gift of homegrown food. I felt so disappointed and I felt like I had let down the very people I had hoped to help.

It seems that many food banks in the UK do not accept fresh food donations. I was told that it was because people don't know how to cook it, but I also think it may have something to do with needing appropriate equipment to store fresh foods without it deteriorating before it's used. Whatever the reason for food banks not accepting fresh food, it was a blow to those gardeners who had taken part and then were unable to give the food to be used to help others.

For future years, I hope to be able to link up with a network or several organisations that can accept homegrown vegetables for use in street food projects or shelters. If I can identify the organisations that can make use of the gifts, then I can point gardeners in the right direction and they can grow some extra food knowing where it will be going at the end of the growing season.

Just before Christmas 2019, I gave the Grow A Gift food that I had grown to a local church who had organised a Christmas day meal for those on their own. It was a larger group of people than in 2018 and I'm not convinced that they had enough of anything to not have to shop for veg too; I gave what I could and felt like I had, at least, done something.

The grass struggled to flourish in the dry conditions

THE NEED FOR RESILIENCE

In stark contrast to the bitterly cold end of winter, the summer of 2018 started in early May and gave us weeks of heat. Not only was it hot, very hot, but it was also dry, relentlessly dry. Parts of the garden began to display signs of stress, of drought and of the poor condition of the soil in the areas to which I hadn't paid enough, or any, attention.

One way to prevent water evaporation from the soil is by using mulch. A layer of organic matter placed on top of the soil, especially damp soil, will help to reduce evaporation and keep the moisture locked safely away in the soil where the plant's roots can access it. It doesn't need to be a deep layer of mulch; just a couple of inches (5cm) can make a difference. My go-to mulching material had been grass clippings because they were free, easily obtainable and on site. The regular mowing of the paddock areas that weren't home to the raised beds provided me with an ongoing supply of mulch. Or it did until the ground became so dry that the grass stopped growing and turned brown!

Some of the raised beds had been mulched, some had plants that were large enough to provide shade to soil below their leaves, others had a relatively high percentage of organic matter in them and they seemed to be able to hold some moisture at the level of the roots even though the soil was very dry on the surface.

A hosepipe ban made me think more carefully about the water collection and storage system at Byther Farm and highlighted the need

It is better to water a smaller area thoroughly than to water a larger area lightly.

When a little and often approach is taken, the roots of the plants will stay near the surface because the water won't penetrate deeply and for those plants to stay alive, they'll need to access that water close to the surface. When you water thoroughly, the liquid will penetrate deeper into the soil with less chance of evaporation and the plant roots will grow down towards it. They will be able to use the nutrients in the deeper levels of the soil and are more likely to find further water at those lower levels. With deeper roots it matters less if the sun or wind dry out the surface of the soil and the plant stands a better chance of survival.

for building in some additional resilience. We already had several water butts collecting rainwater from the building roofs, but the water in those was used up during May, and June and July offered almost no rain to replenish them. The IBC tank and water butts were empty by the end of July.

We gave the chickens and ducks fresh water each day and I used what was left in their buckets at the end of the day to water the garden the next morning. Although we mostly used the shower for washing ourselves, whenever I did have a shallow bath, I kept the water in the bath until the next morning and then scooped it into buckets to water the garden.

The French beans succumbed to the heat of the summer; they produced masses of bean pods, but they were hard and gnarly and not suitable for making a pleasing meal, so I let them grow on to harvest the beans from inside them. The resident wildlife, on the other hand, saw the beans as an ideal meal and within a matter of days, the yellow dwarf beans had been nibbled or snapped open and a huge number of them disappeared entirely. Perhaps those beans were just never destined to be on our dinner table.

When the rain finally arrived at the very end of July, I might have been seen dancing in the rain and skipping around the garden. The sound of the earth soaking up the water was exhilarating and the smell, the petrichor, after those first few rain showers was delightful.

Everything in the garden which up to now had been growing steadily, exploded into a lush, dark green, jungle-like affair.

A YEAR OF FOOD

Following the success of '50 Days of Harvest' in 2017, I decided that during 2018 I would weigh everything that I harvested and foraged for the complete growing year; it would take me right through to late spring of 2019, but it would be good to know exactly how much the garden was capable of producing. The abundance of the harvests during our first two years at Byther Farm had given me confidence in the garden and in nature's ability to provide us with enough food as long as I provided it with sufficient water and nutrients to grow as intensively as I was asking of it.

I weighed all the food grown as it was harvested, although often mangetout (snow peas), strawberries, raspberries and currants were eaten straight from the plants and not weighed. I recorded the daily harvests on the calendar in the kitchen and totalled them at the end of the week.

It was interesting to note the peaks and troughs as different vegetables came into and out of season. I had always imagined that August and September give the highest harvests, but the busiest months were the second half of September through to early November. In part that was due to the squashes being harvested during that period and they had enjoyed the heat of the summer and the rains of August and September to form fruits ranging from large to huge. I also harvested the Greek Gigantes beans, which, rather than being harvested bit by bit through the season, are harvested at the end of the season when the bean pods are full and ripe. Other heavy fruit and veg were harvested during October and November, like apples, pears and sweetcorn, potatoes and cabbages.

By the end of the twelve-month period, I had grown, harvested, gathered and foraged in excess of 2200lbs (1000kg) of nutrient-dense, chemical-free food and enough was stored in the freezers, pantry and in the ground to see us through until

Recording the daily harvest on the kitchen calendar

the harvests started again the next year. Just three years after we started the garden, it looked very much as though we were going to achieve our goal of being mostly self-sufficient in fruit and vegetables, even if at this stage the range of food growing in the garden was not hugely adventurous.

CONSTANT LEARNING

Having just said that we are not hugely adventurous in our eating habits, I do try to avoid predictable repetition. Just as I like to experiment in the kitchen, I like to try new growing methods and vegetables. In the first year at Byther Farm I grew potatoes in the ground after the chickens had scratched through the pile of sawdust, straw and pony and alpaca poop (the slugs ate most of them), the next year I tried growing them under weed-supressing membrane (the slugs still ate a lot of them) and for 2018 I decided to hold a small, highly unscientific trial to see which, if any, of the four mulches I had would give the highest yield.

I planted 12 seed potatoes on a small mound of shop-bought compost and covered three of them with chicken bedding, three with wood chips, three with leaf mould and the last three with homemade compost from the heap.

I treated the whole row in the same way throughout the growing period. I fed the soil a couple of times with comfrey and nettle tea and when I watered, I made sure each section had the same amount of water.

For the first harvest of those potatoes, I lifted one plant from each section to see whether there was any difference in the yield and recorded the weights of the harvest from each plant. I repeated the process for the second and third harvests and we did a taste test.

I knew that different varieties of potatoes tasted different, but we were surprised at the difference in flavour of the potatoes grown under different mulches.

Combined harvest weights

Wood chips	4.86lbs (2206g)
Garden compost	6.41lbs (2910g)
Chicken bedding	7.39lbs (3354g)
Leaf mould	8.17lbs (3706g)

Each year I aim to try a new growing method, medium, a new crop or variety. This is not to be adventurous, but more to expand my knowledge and experience and most importantly, to ensure that I don't become bored with the repetitious annual routine of growing our food. I want to carry on being amazed by nature and the garden. I want to continue to love this thing that keeps me feeling grounded.

Planting seed potatoes for our unscientific trial

Harvesting potatoes

One of the first two birds hatched on our homestead, 4th May 2016

The less than imaginatively named Big White

MOVING PLACES

I had already decided to extend the food forest to cover most of the paddock, so that the trees, shrubs and edible perennials would surround the vegetable garden, providing more shelter and a wider diversity of plants (and harvest), which in turn would encourage a wider variety of wildlife into the garden.

The chickens and turkeys had been living on half of the paddock for three years. Over the last 18 months of that time, I had subdivided their large area into two. One area we called the Diesel field, named after one of the first chickens that came to live with us, and the other was Big White's field.

Big White holds a special place in our hearts. He was one of the first two chicks that we hatched using a small incubator and cemented our desire to raise chickens and ducks for ourselves, rather than to buy poultry for the farm. Big Red was the offspring of Jack (female) and a Cream Legbar cockerel that was here for a few short weeks. The other chick was imaginatively named Big White. I had bought six hatching eggs online of a fairly rare breed called White Jersey Giant.

Jersey Giants are fabulous birds, bred in the USA to be an alternative to turkey; they are large birds with big muscle mass and although we have had cockerels that looked larger than Big White, none of them compared in size when you picked them up. Big White was a chunky chap with a big personality. Jersey Giants are friendly, docile birds and most often have glossy black feathers. White Jersey Giants are slightly smaller than the black, but in my opinion are more beautiful. Between 2016 and 2018 we raised a good breeding flock of White Jersey Giants and sold quite a few birds as well as hatching eggs. They are slow to mature and sometimes it could be 20 weeks or more before I could tell whether the young birds were male or female. It didn't make sense to breed the birds to sell, as the cost of feeding and housing them was almost never covered by the price that people were prepared to pay for them, so I slowly reduced the flock to just two girls and Big White.

There is something almost addictive about raising chickens and certainly I get a huge amount of pleasure from having chicks and ducklings around,

Brahmas

but like so many things, it can easily get out of hand and, almost inevitably, it did.

In early 2017, I posted an advert, of sorts, on the Facebook group of our local community asking whether anyone might be interested in eggs from birds raised on organic feed. I had hoped that we might get a couple or so customers to buy eggs. This would stop us from throwing away surplus eggs and help raise some small funds towards their feed costs. What I hadn't anticipated was over 230 responses saying 'Yes please' to eggs. I didn't need much encouragement to raise more birds and I went on a full-blown chicken hatching spree.

By the end of 2017 we had over 120 chickens, the feed bill had soared and I found it impossible to keep as close an eye on them as I felt was necessary to check their health and wellbeing each day. It turns out that there is a big difference between people saying 'Yes please' to a question online and actually turning up week after week to buy some eggs, but we did have a regular customer base that bought most of the surplus eggs.

As autumn arrived and the chickens went into moult, the number of surplus eggs dwindled, but the chickens still needed to be fed, provided with water and housed safely. So we took the sensible decision to sell some of the young birds and others were sent to freezer camp.

The lesson I took from this experience is that to care for animals to the standard that I think is right, then I need to have few enough birds that I can recognise them as individuals and get to know their idiosyncrasies and behaviours, so that I can tell by looking whether they are behaving differently or seem out of sorts.

We raised several different breeds of chickens to see whether we preferred one to another and without a doubt, there are more breeds that I like than not. I found the Silver-laced Wyandottes like to keep to themselves and the Welsummers didn't seem to be team players. Brahmas are wonderful for their large size and sheer comedic looks; with feather covered legs they look like they are wearing pantaloons – Brahmas in pyjamas! The Cuckoo

Australorps, White Jersey Giants and a few crosses

The flock of
young Australorps

126 YEAR THREE

Marans were delightful, if a little stand-offiish. I came to realise that I prefer big, chunky birds to smaller, delicate ones, and the breed that suited us most were the Australorps. A dual purpose bird, they were large, friendly and superb egg producers giving us eggs almost all year round. I purchased eggs from Australorp breeders (found via the aptly named Australorp Breeders Group on Facebook) and we raised several small batches of chicks.

One hatch was particularly successful; among the chicks were nine lovely little Australorps, their black baby fluff highlighted by grey and white around the tail end. Unfortunately, there were seven males and only two females in this little group, so over the first few months I chose which males would stay and which would go. When I had finally selected the last three males, I spent a great deal of time with them, watching them carefully to understand their individual traits and qualities.

As Australorps grow, they lose the grey and white of the baby fluff and grow glossy black feathers that are so shiny they appear to have a petrol quality. In the sunlight they have a green or purple sheen to the blackness; it's very attractive and was much admired. So, telling these three young males apart wasn't as easy as it might have been and it took time to learn to recognise each of them at a quick glance.

Before too long I had decided that I preferred the look and behaviour of one more than the other two, so he was moved to a separate section of the chicken field with five or six females to settle into a new routine. He was a handsome chap, beautiful even, and we thought he deserved a name. Mr J is very good at choosing nomenclature for the birds we weren't going to name (Jarvis Cockerel was a particularly good one), and this time was no exception.

Maurice-e quickly became a very attentive caretaker of the small group of girls, so much so that he started to get a bit aggressive. I noticed that he would often square shoulders with Big White who was in the area next to his, neatly divided by flexible poultry netting, although it wasn't electrified. The two males would do mirroring behaviour as they sized each other up, but very quickly one of them would seem to get bored and wander off.

One afternoon I went outside to find that Big White and Maurice-e had stopped just looking at each other through the fence; they were having a fight. It was an awful sight there seemed to be blood every-where. Maurice-e was on top of Big White, who was lying on the ground and when I got to them to separate the pair, I saw why. Big White was tangled in the flexible netting and couldn't get away from Maurice-e. My beautiful big white bird was now blood red and I thought he couldn't

Elvis

possibly survive this attack. Mr J managed to get Maurice-e away from Big White and I untangled him from the fencing, scooped him up and took him to the chicken palace, where his house was. In the quiet of this space I wiped away the blood to see how bad his injuries were. I'm not terribly squeamish about cuts and wounds, but I certainly wasn't looking forward to what I might find.

I carefully and gently searched to find the gaping wound that had covered about three-quarters of his feathers in blood. To my amazement, the only injuries that I could find were two or three cuts to his comb and a dented pride. I washed off as much blood as I could and sprayed his comb with the purple spray we kept in the animals' first aid kit. While Big White rested and recovered from his ordeal, we set about creating a neutral zone between the two birds' enclosures to ensure this kind of encounter couldn't happen again.

About a week or so later, Maurice-e was still in a snarky mood and as I went to collect the eggs laid by the girls in his flock, he gave me a look. I told him to be nice and carried on collecting the eggs.

I walked away and as I reached the flexible fencing I felt a sharp pain in the back of my knee, swiftly followed by another pain. Maurice-e was attacking me! It had been a while since I had moved quite so quickly. In one movement I spun round, put down the egg basket, picked up Maurice-e and then put him into his house, firmly locking him in it. Now in tears of surprise and pain, I telephoned Mr J who was in the house and asked him to come to the field. I had already dealt with the immediate threat of further attack from Maurice-e, but I was shaken by the episode and wanted his care and support.

With two violent outbursts in ten days, I knew that we wouldn't be keeping my first choice of Australorp males and looked at the remaining two boys. I chose the larger of the two to replace the badly behaved bird. It seems that I made the right decision; Elvis proved to be popular with his flock and an excellent father to many chicks.

As the year went on, we tried several times to hatch some more ducklings, but it seemed that Frederick had come to the end of his fertile life. To ensure that we would have as many ducks as

Mr Drake behaves like
a gentleman at all times

we'd hoped for throughout the latter part of the year, I looked online at the local poultry group on Facebook and as luck would have it, spotted an advert for eight Aylesbury ducks at a smallholding about 30-40 minutes away. We agreed to purchase them as long as they looked healthy and when we arrived to see them, we were greeted by eight healthy looking, talkative birds.

Travelling in a car with a bunch of large birds in a poultry transit crate is, well, interesting. Duck poop offers an aromatic experience all of its own and it's not one I would rush to recommend to anyone. When we got them home, they headed straight over to the pond we'd made in the duck enclosure and revelled in the fresh clean water and removed the evidence of their journey. In line with our 'no names for livestock' policy, the seven new girls remained nameless, but the drake became Mr Drake. He has been a superb companion for the ducks, tender, watchful and protective and is father and grandfather to many of the ducks we have now.

Back in early 2016, when we got the first small flock of Crested Cream Legbar chickens, the gentleman

that we bought them from told me that he felt anyone who hatched birds should also know how to dispatch birds, so that they are never left to suffer unnecessarily. In my naivety and ignorance, I hadn't really thought about their end of life care; it's easy to be enthusiastic without thinking a thing through to its logical conclusion. And so, in what would have horrified me in my previous roles, I watched videos, read articles and researched the government's advice on humane dispatch of poultry. I didn't want to learn how to do this, but I felt that it was my responsibility to be, as much as possible, prepared for all eventualities.

Mr J and I spent many hours discussing whether, with this new-found knowledge, coupled with the space that we had in the paddock, we should raise some chickens for food. We had been buying organic chicken at the shops for a couple of years and this felt like a natural progression. We would know where our chickens had come from, exactly how they were raised and cared for, what they had eaten and we'd know that they had had a good life.

We bought 15 young birds of a breed that would normally be destined for the supermarket shelves.

There was something slightly grotesque about them; all they seemed to do was eat, sleep and poop. They had grown so rapidly that their feathers didn't seem to have kept up with the speed of expansion of their bodies. We called them The Little Fatties and I couldn't wait to get them outside into the fresh air, onto the grass and under the sun. They responded just as I had hoped; they started to move around more, explore their surroundings and scratch at the grass. They became fairly sociable and the rapid growth slowed enough for them to grow plenty of feathers. These birds have been bred to be dispatched at just a few weeks old and if left too long their bodies can become too heavy for their legs and they become unable to walk. I wanted to avoid this if at all possible and I was delighted that our free-ranging birds kept their leg strength until it was time for them to go to freezer camp.

As time went on, we found we were eating meat less often and smaller portions of it. I wanted more space to grow fruit and vegetables and spend less time on caring for poultry. In late 2018, we made the decision to reduce the chicken numbers to around 30 and so over the next year the bird numbers were reduced and thus the amount of space they required changed. We moved the chickens that lived in the Diesel field to the area under the tall sycamore trees next to the piggery and reduced the size of Big White's field.

Once again, I was thankful that we had used temporary fencing to create the chicken fields and that we had built in flexibility and the capacity for change.

> Don't underestimate the usefulness of flexibility to make changes. Theoretical information is one thing; experience and practice will give a better indication of what's actually needed.

100% homegrown meal

Growing food in the area where the chickens had been living was completely different to the growing in the raised beds of the vegetable garden. Each time we had mucked out the chicken shed, we had spread the bedding onto the Diesel field and the chickens had been working it into the top couple of inches of soil for some time. The soil was a joy to work with; I planted several rows of potatoes, but not much else as I was still focussing on other areas of the garden. Soil that is so rich in nitrogen produces tall leafy plants. By the end of the growing season we had a good potato crop. We also had masses of waist high weeds.

Once again, I felt overwhelmed by the amount of work it would take to keep on top of the weeds to have a pristine garden like those that I've seen in photographs in gardening books. Talking this through with Mr J, he suggested that I stop setting myself impossible targets and re-evaluate what is most important to me in the garden – everything looking pretty or growing food while I was also still developing the area. It was time for another rethink and reframe of my thought process. I turned the feeling of being overwhelmed around and began looking at those weeds as a source of green material for the compost heaps.

With a renewed outlook and spring in my step, I tackled the weeds, sorting through them to put annual weeds in the compost heap and perennial weeds into thick plastic sacks to tie the tops and stack in a corner to allow them to rot down before returning them to the soil at a later date. There were a lot of bags of rotting pernicious weeds hidden away under the hedge that year.

I'm not very good at keeping up with the weeding. I don't hoe them all away when they are tiny because firstly, I don't always think about doing that and secondly, because a part of me wants to see what is growing in case there are seedlings of plants that I want, that I could transplant to elsewhere in the garden. I love free plants and I don't like the thought of accidentally hoeing away a small treasure. I have lovingly lifted and moved dozens of self-sown, volunteer viola from the gravel yard and countless herb and flowers from the beds and wood chip paths. Learning what young plants look like is valuable knowledge and with such a large garden to fill, it has saved us hundreds of pounds.

But there's a fine line between allowing seedlings to grow enough to be able to identify them and letting them grow so much that they flower and go to seed and spread even further around the garden. I guess it's a case of finding a happy medium and also being prepared to live in a less than pristine environment.

> Understand your priorities and revisit them often to help prevent feeling overwhelmed by less important tasks.

FOR THE LOVE OF BEETS

2018 was the year of the beetroot. I grew the round roots of Bolthardy and long roots of Cylindra and despite the lack of rain in the earlier part of the summer, the beetroots grew incredibly well. I tried a white beetroot called Albina Veraduna; the smooth white round roots were slightly sweeter in taste and we both liked them. We also tried Chioggia; when it is cut through, it has pink and white stripes in concentric circles and a delightful taste.

I will happily eat a few slices of pickled beetroot, but Mr J isn't very keen. We do, however, both like roasted beetroot and after seeing a recipe on a cooking programme, I cooked beetroot steak. Thick slices of beetroot are slowly fried over a low heat in a frying pan with a fat of your choice. We used duck fat which gave the beetroot a rich taste and I've used olive oil and that has worked equally well.

I also made some beetroot wine. It didn't taste like beetroot at all, but it did have notes of fruity earthiness. Mr J didn't like it for drinking and I no longer drink alcohol, so I used it in cooking and it might just be the best cooking wine we've ever had. I will make more in the future, so that we have it to add its rich vegetable-y taste to stews and casseroles. It was also a great conversation piece when friends came to visit.

GARDEN VISITORS & BUILDING FRIENDSHIPS

During that summer, I invited some new friends that I'd met via YouTube to visit Byther Farm. Of course, I hadn't actually met them before, but we had talked at length online. In June, Erica (*Erica's Little Welsh Garden*) joined me to remove a laburnum tree and clear the weeds from the gravelled courtyard behind the kitchen. In a moment of unrivalled imagination, we named this area the 'kitchen courtyard garden'. Using the wonders of modern technology, we broadcast our activities live on her YouTube channel, including the moment that Erica decided to open an outhouse door and see what was inside it.

I had warned her that we had only opened this particular door once during the previous three years and I knew what was inside! Before we moved here it was an outdoor loo, but the previous owners had removed it and emptied the space as part of their renovations of the property. The small room was not entirely empty; a community of humongous spiders had moved in. Although I warned her, Erica still felt the need to open the door and peek inside.

Chioggia beetroots have pink and white concentric circles

As bold as a bold thing, she forced the door open and looked about. What happened next seemed to go in cartoon-like slow motion. At the same time as she let out a loud shriek, she leapt about six feet away from the door and promptly started laughing.

This incident cemented our friendship and we have laughed together most days since. We find the same things ridiculous, share a passion for gardening and support each other in our videography endeavours. When she got married, I spent the fortnight beforehand making jam from homegrown fruit from Erica's and our garden, for her to use as place markers on the wedding guests' tables. I was delighted and felt honoured to be invited to attend her wedding. I took my camera and made an unofficial wedding video for her as a gift.

In late August, Tony O'Neill (*Simplify Gardening*) visited and we filmed two videos, one for my channel and one to be published on his channel. Tony has visited us on several occasions, often to tackle a specific task with me, or for me, and I have visited Tony's allotment plot to film, to help out and just to spend time in the company of a good friend. Our first visit to Tony's plot was well-timed; he had just harvested a huge crop of grapes from his polytunnel. He gave us sweet, white grapes for eating and two over-filled carrier bags of red grapes with which to make wine and jelly. I have returned a few of the grapes to Tony in glass containers.

During one visit, I helped Tony to clear some of the weeds and overgrowth from his fruit plot as he was going to move all the plants and fruit trees to a new plot that he has just acquired. As we scooped up armful after armful of a particularly badly behaved bindweed, I heard a helicopter overhead. I wondered to myself where it was; I paused and looked skyward, but I couldn't see it anywhere. The hum got louder and still I couldn't see helicopter. As I looked around the penny finally dropped that it wasn't a helicopter, it was a buzzing nest.

Erica and I filming our first video together

Making jam for Erica's wedding was a privilege

Many cups of tea have been consumed in the shed at Tony's allotment plot

Recording the first of many videos with Huw

Wasps had made a home among the weeds and we were close to gathering an armful of disturbed, angry wasps. I did my usual best in these circumstances and walked away as briskly as I could, quietly hoping that Tony wouldn't realise that I was running.

In September, Huw Richards (*Huw Richards*) came to film a video collaboration that we had been planning for almost seven months. We had originally planned for him to visit Byther Farm in June, but other commitments meant that he had had to rearrange. In hindsight, I am so glad that his visit was postponed because the garden looked so much better; the summer of sunshine had kept my spirits lifted and having met Erica and Tony previously, I felt less awkward or shy about meeting another YouTube content creator. At the time Huw's YouTube channel had around 90,000 subscribers, while mine had just 3,750 and try as I might, I felt more than a little star struck.

Huw and I recorded two videos for use on our channels and we agreed to publish them simultaneously in a few days' time. In the afternoon we visited Ragmans Lane Farm in the Forest of Dean to each film another video for our respective channels.

The most surprising thing about that day was seeing the small-holding through his eyes. Working here day in and day out, I had, to some extent, become blind to its charm and to how much had been achieved in the first couple of years. Huw's enthusiasm and encouragement helped me to appreciate once again how abundant the garden was becoming.

It didn't take very long to realise that although from different generations (I'm just about old enough to be his grandmother), we look at the world in similar ways and we have enough in common to have formed a firm friendship.

During that first visit and several subsequent trips to Byther Farm, Huw helped out by moving some wood chips from the front garden, where the small orchard is, to further into the food forest. On one occasion, he moved a huge volume of wood chips to a double size compost bay outside the run where some young turkeys were living. Each and every time he dumped a wheelbarrow full of chippings into the compost bay, the turkeys shouted their high-pitched gobbling noise at him and Huw calmly responded with a comment or two for them. For about 40 minutes he went back and forth with more wood chips and with each round of the conversation, the turkeys were slightly louder or more persistent with their heckling.

Through social media I have made many new friends. A few have visited us, others we have been to visit, yet more we have met at events like Abergavenny Food Festival, Royal Welsh Spring Festival and Malvern Spring and Autumn Shows. By far the largest number of new acquaintances and friends live in other countries. Across the globe I have found connections with fellow gardeners, homesteaders, video- and film-makers and enjoy being a part of these more distant communities.

Technology allows me to communicate quickly and in real time with friends on other continents, sharing our similarities and learning about the differences in social, cultural and gardening or growing practices. For the last three years, I have chatted using a video messaging service similar to texting, but using video to relay the messages. Through this I've developed good friendships with YouTube content creators like Trish (*Willow Creek Homestead*) and Lorella (*Lorella – Plan Bee Orchard and Farm*); both families live in Missouri, USA, and we share our ups and downs on a regular basis. These purely online friendships will change dynamics in the future as Lorella and I have planned that she will visit us at Byther Farm in the next year and if I ever feel that I could cope with travelling such a distance, I will visit both of them at their homes.

I also keep in regular and close contact with my sister and almost daily contact with my daughter. Both of whom, if they weren't family, I would choose to have as close friends.

Build social networks and nurture friendships – life on a smallholding can be isolating. You may spend much of your day alone, but it's not necessary to feel lonely.

VERTICAL POTENTIAL – ABOVE GROUND

There's a point in the year at which the garden suddenly seems to become very full, looking lush and productive. It happens around the time when the climbing bean plants reach the top of their supports, so that I can no longer look across the length of the garden uninterrupted.

I decided this year to try growing more plants vertically, adding more height and structure to the shape of the vegetable garden. I found a short roll of pig netting, an off-cut given to us by a neighbour, and I propped it between two of the raised beds to see if it would be long enough to make an arch. I pushed bamboo canes and a length of wood

Spaghetti squash grows, climbing over a makeshift arch

into the raised bed on one side and fixed them to the bean support structure in that bed, making a fairly robust and sturdy support for the pig netting. Mr J hammered two more lengths of wood into the far side of the next raised bed, creating the supports for a long and slightly wobbly growing arch.

I planted two spaghetti squash plants in the raised bed where the beans were also growing, in the hope that they would climb up the new pig netting support and make use of the vertical space.

At the base of the other side of this arch I planted two Blue Banana squash to scramble up this vertical growing space and hopefully meet the spaghetti squash in the middle of the arch, over our heads, to create an attractive growing display.

The Blue Banana squash were disappointing in their growth, but they did produce a few fruits. I think they were less vigorous in growth than I had hoped because, rather than plant them into the soil, I planted them into growing bags and I suspect they were unable to access enough nutrients. Another lesson was learnt. I had used the growing bags because that side of the archway went into a bed that had been filled with weeds at the end of the year before and I hadn't as yet cleared the weeds and mulched the bed. I was cutting corners and the harvest reflected my lack of preparation of the growing space.

The spaghetti squash, on the other hand, were a complete success. They scrambled up the pig netting archway as I regularly threaded the growing tips back and forth through the spaces in the netting and they produced large, tasty fruits. I harvested 18 spaghetti squash from the two plants; half of them were harvested earlier in the summer before they had developed their hard, yellow skins. I cooked the squash and froze it in portion size packs for use later in the year. Had I known at the time just how well spaghetti squash can store in a cool and not-humid room in the house, I could have saved myself the work. Once the squashes are ripe, they can be left in a dry, airy place for their skins to cure to the stage where a fingernail, pressed against the skin, will not cause a mark and then they will happily store without the need for preserving for 12 months or more if necessary.

Following the success of the squash archway, I decided that for future years I would make more use of vertical space for growing squashes; all I needed to do was create suitable support structures for them.

I still cut corners in early summer when there are so many plants to get into the ground within a short space of time and every year I am disappointed by the results.

As time goes on and more of the garden space is developed, the work required on the beds is tending and mulching, rather than creating and soil-building. Fewer plants are put into the ground in a hurriedly made hole and more are being planted into ground that is rich in organic matter with a healthy balance of microorganisms.

I spend quite a lot of time imagining what the garden might look like, how it could function more efficiently and dreaming of it being lush, green and fruitful with a minimum of input from me. They say it's good to have dreams. There comes a point when the dreaming needs to be set aside and when realistic plans are made for the practical work that needs to be done to turn the reality into the imagined growing space.

As I brought in the harvests during late 2018, I started to think less about concepts and ideas and more about the practical steps that would need to be taken to turn the rest of the paddock into a productive food forest. The lists reappeared. Lists of what needed doing, moving, changing, reorganising. Lists of materials and their alternatives and somewhere in the middle of all of that planning and organising, the earth fell out from under my feet.

A hole appeared in the front garden and driveway

VERTICAL POTENTIAL – BELOW GROUND

During the summer a small section of our driveway had dropped in level and given that it had been so hot and dry for a sustained period, I assumed that the earth had contracted and formed a shallow hollow in that spot. During October, the small dip started to grow and it grew at an alarming rate.

Over the course of two weeks it went from being about 8 inches (20cm) across, 2 feet (60cm) long and 2 inches (5cm) deep to around 15-16 feet (5m) across, 20 feet (6m) long and 5 feet (1.5m) deep. I made the mistake of searching online for 'sinkhole'.

Mr J and I lay in bed at night, unable to sleep with worry, listening for creaking and groaning noises as the ground slowly opened up. We were terrified that the hole would suddenly enlarge during the night and engulf the house, burying us alive in a seemingly bottomless pit. I cannot express how scared we both were at what the future held for us. Our homes should be a sanctuary, a place where we can retreat and feel safe and secure, but the expanding hole in front of our house had taken away that feeling and left us feeling vulnerable, alarmed and frightened.

Over the course of a week or so, the hole in the ground became more defined

One night in response to a dull thud, Mr J leapt out of bed and flung the window open, staring into the inky blackness of the night. He's not sure what he expected to see; he was unlikely to be able to make out a dark hole in the unlit driveway of an unlit garden that is away from the lights of the main road. Glued to the spot in fear of the unknown changes in our garden, he was joined by Monty, who had been asleep under the bed and, we think, as he woke up and stretched, had banged against one of the boxes stored under the bed. Our fear was allowing our imaginations to get the better of us.

In response to this crisis I had sprung into action, which is my usual coping mechanism. Do, do, do and don't stop to think for too long; try to gain some control of the uncontrollable situation.

I spoke to the council to ask whether there had been any sinkholes reported in the past and was told none that they knew of (although later we learnt that they had filled in and repaired several shallow holes that had, over the years, appeared in the fields surrounding us, but the member of staff I spoke to didn't know about them).

I spoke to our insurance company who seemed very slow to respond to my increasingly panic-stricken phone calls. After about 10 days, when the hole was now causing us concern about getting the car in and out of the driveway, the insurance company sent someone to come and have a look at it.

At this point neither we nor the man from the insurance company saw any evidence of any damage to our house and we were informed that the insurance policy didn't cover an exploratory investigation of the cause of the hole because our house wasn't in danger of damage. This was good news and bad news! We were mightily relieved that the hole was unlikely to damage (or consume) the house, but worried about how we would pay for the investigations needed and the repair of the area. What we did know was that we couldn't just leave it and do nothing as it was still getting larger in width and length.

Worryingly, every couple of days a new crack would appear in the soil and driveway around the edge of the hole and the new section would slide into the hole; our only comfort was that it didn't appear to be getting any deeper.

Relaying my fears to my sister, who lives a few miles away, she said that she would ask her neighbours to speak to us. They were geotechnical experts and for a living spent their time looking into holes in the ground. A few emails later and they had agreed to visit our home and do an initial assessment of the work that might be needed and a guesstimate of the

Monty – who, me?

The ground cracked and a new section slid into the hole

Eventual size of the hole in the ground marked in orange

costs involved. At some point I got it into my head that we might need to find £20,000 to £40,000. They assured us that, depending on what was found below ground, it could be sorted out for less.

Mr J and I talked through all the options we could think of to raise money. Would we need to take out a loan or mortgage? Would we even get a loan secured against the house with a big hole in the ground just in front of it? Could we afford the repayments if we did get a loan? What impact would a loan have on our lifestyle? Would Mr J have to work full time rather than the part time hours he did now? How could I earn more from the farm? We both felt sick, physically sick with worry about the hole in the ground and the hole in our finances. We considered a GoFundMe appeal, but felt we needed to know the cost of investigation and repairs first. All the while we wanted to get this issue resolved without asking others for help with money.

The visiting geotechnical experts reassured us that our house was not at risk and that even if the hole was to suddenly increase in depth it would only go a few metres as the substructure of the soil and rock was X amount ... I didn't really understand what was being said, but I was reassured that we weren't going to have a 100 feet (30m) deep hole open up in the driveway.

They explained that it would need to be excavated back to the rock (fortunately, not very far below the surface) and then filled with something to make it safe and sturdy enough to cover back over with soil.

This was possibly the bleakest period that we've had since moving here. The light levels were poor, we were heading into winter, my mood was dropping and we were desperately worried about the hole in the ground. It was the start of the busy season in Mr J's job and he was working more and more hours and coming home to find me in a crumpled heap. And somewhere in that messy chaos I felt something shift.

I remembered the idea that the answer is in the problem, so I tried to find some positives in what felt like a horrible situation. If we had to get all that work done, perhaps there were some other ways to use the even larger hole that they would be creating. I thought about an outdoor swimming pool, but it was too close to the gate and front of the house to offer any privacy. We could use it for a duck pond, but the ducks make such a mess. Then I hit on the idea of using part of the excavated hole to create an underground greenhouse. All we would need to do would be put concrete sides and floor in and then we could have a glass roof fitted on it. Steps from the drive could lead down to a door. I ignored the fact that we didn't have any money for the exploratory work or the repairs; I focussed on how this would be a fabulous way to make something good from such a bad situation.

The hole had become large enough to engulf two inspection covers for the water supply to our property, so I rang the County Council once again and said that I was concerned that it could impact on the water supply. Our water is supplied by the County Council as the property used to belong to them. A couple of days later, the Estates and Farms Manager from the County Council arrived. He took a brief look around and said that he'd send a team to check that the water pipes hadn't been damaged.

The following four days went by like a surreal dream. Men arrived with listening equipment and spades. They showed me how you can hear water flowing underground by placing a tube onto the ground and putting your ear on the top of the pipe. And yes, we could hear flowing water.

The workmen reappeared with diggers and safety equipment to further investigate. They found pipes coming on to the property, pipes leading away, pipes going to the house and pipes going around the house – it was like the Piccadilly Circus of underground pipework. They also found the cause of the big hole in the garden and driveway.

At some point the mains water inlet pipe had not been secured properly or during the hot weather as the soil had dried out, the capping to one part of the pipework had shifted. Whatever had caused it, there was now a constant jet of water gushing into the ground at mains water pressure and it had washed away so much soil under the surface, that the top had collapsed.

It was not a sinkhole. It was a washout.

Not only was it a washout, but the County Council agreed to cover all the costs of investigation and repairs and to make good all the damage the gushing pipes had done.

A veritable army of workmen appeared (at least six of them) with diggers and trucks with trailers and they opened up the hole and dug down to a depth where the subsoil layers were dry and compacted. They mended the broken pipework, fitted new water meters in an easily accessible place and removed redundant pipework. Then they filled the hole back in with hardcore and rubble and even buried three large lumps of concrete that had been here when we moved in. After the rubble they filled the top 2-3 feet (60-90cm) with soil and replaced the gravel on the driveway.

A year later you can just about make out where the hole was in the front garden, but on the driveway it is an invisible mend; only our memories and a few photographs are left of that horrid, stressful time. I know that I continue to say that I like a project to focus on during the autumn and winter months, but I'd rather not have that kind of a project again!

Dealing with how we felt and what we did during this period was an eye-opener for me. It made me realise how fiercely independent we had become and how, when faced with a relative disaster, we were searching for the positives. I was looking at the problem to become the solution.

EVALUATING AND PLANNING

As part of the ongoing evaluation process, each year during early December, Mr J and I sit down to evaluate how the growing year has been, what we would like to change completely or just do a little differently.

Potentially it could be a brutal process of self-destructive negativity, but we have both learnt to be kind to ourselves about things that haven't worked, especially if they are beyond our control, and to celebrate the successes. We talk generally, then in a more focussed way, then narrow it down to each area of the homestead. This year, there was plenty to celebrate and much to get excited about for the year ahead.

Mid December 2018

- ▸ How well or not did the crops grow? What do we want more of? What don't we like and won't grow again next year?
- ▸ How many chickens and ducks do we want to raise next year? Do we want turkeys or guinea fowl again?
- ▸ How much did each of us enjoy the growing year? Did we enjoy the tasks that we assigned ourselves or each other?
- ▸ Which maintenance tasks do we need to do urgently, attend to soon and get done at some point over the next year or so?
- ▸ What will be the main projects for the year ahead? In what order do they need tackling? Do we have the resources for them? Or the skills? Or knowledge?
- ▸ What has inspired us, what do we aspire to and what are our dreams?

Some of these discussions rumble on for days or even weeks as we toss ideas back and forth and use each other as a sounding board. Sometimes the ideas that seemed so good at first, fall by the wayside as we start to see the pitfalls or impracticalities.

Other ideas that are said almost in jest are developed, explored, mulled over and eventually agreed upon. 2018 was a year of research and of deciding to take the next step in growing food – some for us, some to give away and some to sell to create a small income.

As we passed our third anniversary of moving here and I was settled and comfortable that we were well and truly in a rhythm that worked for us, I felt ready to take the next step in the healing process that was happening all around me. I finally felt able to tackle the excess weight that I had been carrying around for the last few years. The prolonged, excessive heat of the summer of 2018 had been uncomfortable and I felt as though I had lumbered my way around the gardens for most of the year. The additional strain of carrying so much weight was bound to be taking its toll on my hips and knees because they hurt most of the time and my feet and ankles were constantly swollen, not just from the heat, but from the extra pressure they were under.

Having made the decision to lose some weight, on 28th December 2018 I asked Mr J to drive me to a local weight loss group and I made a commitment to be kinder to myself over the coming months and years.

Carrots   beetroots   rhubarb   chard   Taunton Deane kale
parsley   mint   chives   marjoram
thyme   tarragon   savory   strawberries
walking onions   lemon balm   lettuce   raspberries
potatoes   peas   red cabbage   lovage   turnips   runner beans
French beans   borlotti beans   basil   broad (fava) beans
calabrese   dill   courgette (zucchini)   swedes (rutabaga)
squashes   rosehips   apples   pears
nasturtiums   calendula   radish   Greek gigantes beans
sweetcorn   lettuce   salad leaves
beet leaves   tomatoes   cucumbers   basil   spring onions   melon

Squashes curing in the fresh air

Salsify seed
heads look like
giant dandelions

YEAR FOUR

2019

HENCE SPRINGS OUR HOPE

MORE OF THE SAME, BUT DIFFERENT

Having moved many of the chickens to the area under the sycamore trees by the piggeries, we had just one small flock left in the paddock. We planned to have turkeys again, but this year they would live in an enclosed area that led out from the chicken palace; I couldn't face another year of pleading with turkeys to come down from the barn roof. The relocation of the birds gave me a new area into which I planned to extend the food forest. But I also felt that there was something missing, that the whole paddock area was lacking a focal point, something that pulled the elements together. I wanted some frivolity among the utilitarian landscape. After three years of focussing on creating a space to produce food, I wanted the lightness and frippery of flowers for the sake of flowers.

So, in my usual, rough-sketch style of planning, I had an idea of where I might put some flower beds and also where eventually I might put a polytunnel.

In late winter 2018 and early spring 2019, I created an archway tunnel from a simple polytunnel kit we bought on the local community recycling page on Facebook. It was too low for the purpose I had in mind, so I hammered metal posts into the ground and strapped the uprights of the archway to the posts to raise it well above head height. As I was concerned that the wind would buffet against it and pull it out of the ground; deep raised beds constructed around the metal posts offered more stability. I fixed some metal grid panels to the archway and some pig netting that we were given by my sister for climbing plants to cling to as they grew.

Beneath the archway tunnel I laid a wide pathway using weed suppressing membrane and wood chips. Before the planting softened the hard lines, it looked like an airport runway cutting through the length of the paddock.

More raised beds were built around the sides of a pinched rectangle and although I filmed making this new garden area, I only shared the videos with my supporters on Patreon. Mr J suggested that I call this area the Patrons' Garden.

In early March, after so many years of wanting one, we took delivery of a polytunnel kit for a 14 feet (4.27m) wide by 30 feet (9.1m) long polytunnel.

Our friend Tony O'Neill helped us put the polytunnel kit together and left us for a week or so to dig out a trench all around the frame which the polytunnel cover would be buried in to make it secure.

Burying the polytunnel cover

Digging out the trench about a spade's depth deep and around one foot (30cm) wide was no mean feat. Having worked in the soft compost of the raised beds for the last three years, I had forgotten just how clay-filled and stony the ground of the paddock actually was. Mr J and I took it in turns to dig a little at a time and after a few days, Mr J spent a couple of early evenings on it and completed the task.

Tony returned to help us put the cover onto the frame and bury the sides of the plastic covering in the trench that we had dug out.

After the polytunnel was erected and complete, I was beside myself with excitement. It felt like now I was a 'proper' gardener. This was nonsense of course, and a self-imposed label.

Once the pathway around the polytunnel was completed I knew how much space I had left in the Patrons' Garden and I created the last of the raised beds for that area. It sits parallel to the full long side of the polytunnel. I had visions of an espalier structure in it, with fruit trees trained along the wires, to soften the look of the polytunnel as we looked across the food forest towards the fields beyond. But not wanting to waste the space until such time as we had that organised, I planted the entire 4 feet (1.2m) by 24 feet (7.3m) bed with potatoes.

As I harvested the potatoes later in the year, I replaced each potato plant with an ornamental herbaceous plant. I bought reasonably large plants from a local nursery for approximately £10 each; much more than I would usually pay for a herbaceous plant. They generally grow so quickly that I can't justify paying this kind of price, but I had a plan.

When I got home, I divided each of the plants into several smaller clumps or pieces. As luck would have it, most of the plants were so healthy that I was able to divide them into 5-10 pieces. Some of them I grew on in pots before planting out and others were planted direct into the border.

Large plants were divided and each section planted into pots

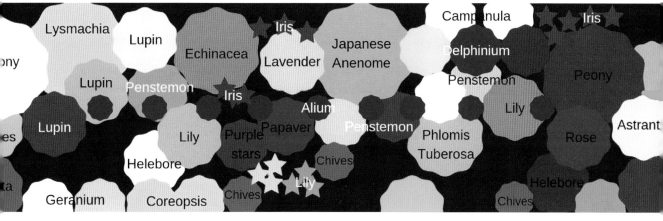

The Long Bed planting plan

This allowed me to plant up a much larger area in this bed and it cost less than buying a similar number of smaller plants.

Looking at the border now, I can see that most of the flowers were planted later in the year and that it would benefit from a selection of spring and early summer plants to give it year-round interest.

'The Long Bed' was carefully planned for interest for most of the year. Non-edible flowering plants with a variety of colours and textures as well as a long flowering period. Although as yet there are still some plants that I haven't sourced for this bed, there are others that I have been given that have filled those spaces. As with any garden, it is an ever-evolving space that I've really enjoyed creating.

In the 'Edible Flower Bed' I selected plants for their edible properties as well as their visual appeal.

'The Wide Border' runs parallel to the polytunnel and will, over time, mature and soften the view towards the polytunnel.

I also made a crude hügelkultur bed by moving some partially rotted tree trunks to make the edges of the bed. A few more, slightly smaller logs were placed in the centre of the space and several broken and partly rotted, heat-treated pallets were added. I filled the gaps between broken pallets and logs with wood chips, duck bedding and bought-in compost from the local green waste recycling business. It is located under a silver birch tree that my daughter gave to me for Mother's Day the first year we lived here. It was about 8 inches high when it arrived by post and I am delighted that it has grown into such a handsome tree that casts its dappled shade onto the bed below. I call this bed the Cottage Border.

During early 2019, I received a delightful email. The sender said that she had been searching on YouTube for videos about permaculture and had spotted one about a local farm designed and run on a permaculture basis. She was surprised and pleased to find that it was my video about Ragmans Lane Farm. She wanted to offer her time here for a day, on a voluntary basis, and hoped that I would be happy to talk to her about the work I had done to date at Byther Farm. The sender of the email was none other than the purchaser of my parents' former home.

We arranged a day for her to visit and I tentatively suggested that she might bring some small cuttings or divisions of some of the plants from my parents' garden, many of which I had given to my parents over 30 years ago. She was happy to oblige and arrived with several plants, roots and cuttings that now live in the Cottage Border and remind me of my parents whenever I walk past them.

The Patrons' Garden has added a sense of completeness and maturity to the whole paddock. I grew cosmos from seed to add fast-growing height, fullness and a riot of colour and planted them in the Wide Border and Cottage Border. The huge daisy shaped flowers were regularly covered with pollinators.

It was only after I had completed the Patrons' Garden that I realised how much I had been undervaluing the role that flowers play in my garden, as well as the part they play in lifting my spirits. The bright, airy splashes of colour could be seen from almost every spot in the food forest and vegetable garden, and for the few months while the beds were filled with colour, I felt a deep-rooted, nourishing sense of joy.

FLOWERS FOR FOOD

In previous years I have grown calendula, borage and chives to use their flowers in salads and they are very much a vital part of the vegetable garden. The few perennial flowers put into the failed herbaceous border in the first year had been moved to a small holding space and now that the Patrons' Garden was echoing their colours in a big display, the garden looked more cohesive.

Since I started gardening in my own garden in the early 1980s, I have always had roses and peonies and this home is no different. I brought rose cuttings with me and my dear friend Jane, who has helped me in every garden I've created, gave me a beautiful, scented rose from her garden.

It wasn't until recently that I started looking at roses as a potential food source and using rosehips in our kitchen. I have vague recollections of trying to make rosehip syrup when I was in my teens or early twenties; I don't know what came of it as I don't recall drinking any. I now gather rosehips from our hedges and from the roses dotted across the whole site to make rosehip wine, to which Mr J is rather partial. Rosehips are collected and stored in the freezer until I have enough to make wine; this takes the pressure off me having to make wine immediately or to mix the rosehips with another fruit if I haven't gathered enough hips in one go.

As I continue to learn about the use of flowers in the kitchen, I plan to include more of them in the garden. I recently read that dried calendula flowers can be used in cooking as a replacement for saffron to add colour and a gentle taste to ingredients like rice. Discoveries like this are exciting because it means one less ingredient that would have been purchased in a shop and one more use of a plant that we grow in abundance.

Calendula and nasturtiums are now used in the kitchen

What A Wise Mother Knows

My mother was a funny old girl, private to the extreme and I never really got to know her very much as a person. We spent great swathes of time together, in her home, in my home, out for lunch, at the gym and we went on holiday together (out of choice!). For her last two years we spent a goodly chunk of the day together every day and yet still, she never offered to share much of herself with me.

This morning I had a big wave of missing mum, I had made a batch of scones for elevenses and as I sat and ate a couple (or three) of them, I thought about mum.

Mum suffered from depression for many years and most days when we got home from school she was in bed, curtains drawn and not wanting to see anyone. But as we got older and her spirits lifted (the two may have been connected, but I don't think so) we saw more of her. She was an excellent cook and a progressive one too. I remember her introducing us to this fancy new food from Italy called pizza when I was about nine years old. My parents had held a fundraising 'at home' lunch and she made pizza from scratch; most of the people there didn't know what it was. How enlightened and globally aware we were in the early seventies! To this day I haven't met anyone who can make roast potatoes as good as mum's were, nor lemon meringue pie as tangy, rich and sticky, although her experiment with rice pudding topped with jam and meringue was never a favourite of mine.

She had promised to share with me her secret recipe for egg custard, her version of a large crème caramel, but she didn't and so that fabulous recipe has gone with her.

But she did share some valuable life lessons with me and here are some of them (please don't take any of these as good advice; they are simply things that my mother used to say often).

Mum and I in Bristol, March 2012

- Expect less of other people, then you won't feel disappointed. She also advised me to expect more of other people because folks often rise to the challenge.

- Cook with love in your heart; it makes the food taste better.

- Always bake small cakes (fairy cakes) when the children aren't home; they can have some when they get back, but in the meantime they don't know that you've eaten a load of them yourself.

- Your house doesn't need to be clean to be welcoming; a warm smile that comes from the heart is worth a thousand cans of furniture polish.

- Practise making chocolate bon bons or petit fours about a month before Christmas, make at least three batches before the final one. And it's best not to tell anyone that you made the practice ones, just eat them.

- If you iron nothing else, iron your pillow-cases; it makes the bed look properly made and feels nicer when you get into bed.

- Teach your family that the drawer of your bedside table is out of bounds. Then keep your chocolate in it.

- If a job's worth doing well, it's probably worth paying someone who knows what they're doing to do it for you.

- Small cuts, grazes, bumps and bruises can all be made better by a bit of mother's spit on a tissue applied to the affected area.

- Guilt-free food contains no calories.

(Disclaimer: This is not a list of advice, nor is much of it accurate; it is purely a list of things my mother used to say.)

Excerpt from 6th August 2016

DEVELOPMENT AND LEARNING

There have been other delightful discoveries. Watching a video on Huw Richards' YouTube channel, highlighting the work of a permaculturist in Scotland, I had a bit of a lightbulb moment. In turn this led to a major shift in mindset about a problem that I've been struggling with for four years.

Swathes of the paddock, that are now the food forest and market garden area, are peppered with sturdy, determined dock plants that, despite my best efforts to dig them up and exclude light from them, have resolutely returned, almost mocking my efforts to remove them.

The main reason for the robustness of these plants is the long tap root that they send deep into the soil, anchoring them firmly into the ground. There are other plants, like comfrey, that I grow because of their potential as highly nutrient dense food for plants, using it to chop and drop around trees and shrubs and to make comfrey tea.

What I saw on the video was that dock leaves were being used in the same way: a chop and drop mulch that would add nutrients from deep in the soil to the plants growing in the shallower layers of soil. And in that moment, I suddenly realised that I didn't have a dock problem; I had another plentiful source of nutrients to feed the plants I do want to grow.

This potential for learning, the constant flow of ideas that challenge my preconceptions, is one of the things that draws me to gardening and to working with nature, rather than against it. It's often said, but I find proven true time and again, 'the more I know, the more I realise that I don't know'. The type of knowledge that liberates me from something I have been struggling with, is powerful and empowering and those lightbulb moments when we can suddenly see issues in a new way are, I feel, the best of all.

I always think that winter is the time that I learn the most, during the times when my energy isn't being used in the garden or in processing food in the kitchen, but learning is a constant process, from learning about new plants or planting methods to trying to work out why a crop failed or how to use a new piece of equipment. It's all a learning process, but I don't necessarily see it as that at the time.

In winter, I make a conscious effort to study a specific subject or new area of knowledge and it is often done through a formal learning method, albeit nowadays online.

Squirrel hole in old plum tree

During 2016, I spent quite a while looking for an Introduction to Permaculture course, and because I had no income it needed to be free of charge. I found one via Oregon State University. I sped through the course, hungry for the information and to gain an insight into and understanding of the practices I had been doing in the garden over the years. Methods that I had been using because they made sense to me and seemed to work were explained and the technical and more scientific explanations were fascinating. I found myself thinking 'see, I knew I wasn't mad to be doing x, y or z'.

In autumn 2017, I found a free Permaculture Design Course; it didn't offer a certificate at the end of the 72 hour course, but it did offer me access to more information. I struggled with the course, the videos were up to an hour long at a time and I kept falling asleep during them. The passive nature of watching a video and answering three or four questions at the end of it just wasn't working for me, but I continued on as I wanted the nuggets of knowledge it contained. One of the problems I find with this passive learning method is that although I have the time to watch videos in the winter, I don't take the information on board; it just doesn't stay in my brain for very long. Having snoozed my way through over 50 hours of the course, I resigned myself to being

defeated by it and started to look for another course that might help me to learn in a way that was engaging and would help me retain the precious knowledge that I wanted so badly. And then spring arrived and my time was filled with gardening once more.

In a local charity shop I spotted and bought a copy of *Food Not Lawns* by Heather Jo Flores. I'm not the fastest reader, but I was so inspired by what I was reading that it only took a week to read through and thoroughly enjoy. A quick search on the internet revealed that Heather Jo was offering a free Emotional Permaculture course. I signed up for it and a whole new set of learning opportunities opened up.

Following the Emotional Permaculture course, I signed up for a free year-long permaculture course from the Permaculture Women's Guild. Small bite-size lessons are delivered to my email inbox weekly and they are engaging, thought-provoking and have practical exercises to carry out. The Permaculture Women's Guild also offers a full Permaculture Design Certificate (PDC) course that is delivered by over 40 women from across the globe. Knowing the style of learning offered by the courses, I was keen to sign up, but finding the finances for the course was a big hurdle to overcome.

In the meantime, I had contacted Heather Jo to ask if I could interview her for a video on my YouTube channel. It took us around six months to organise it and find a time when we were both available and in the right frame of mind, but eventually we talked on a video call and agreed for Heather Jo to film her responses to my questions. We also talked about the PDC and to my surprise and delight, she invited me to consider becoming a tutor for the course. To be a tutor, I would definitely need to have the Certificate, after all how could I support other people's learning without having completed the course myself?

The marvellous system of bartering came into play again and I agreed to undertake some work for the Permaculture Women's Guild in lieu of a cash payment for the course. I am currently working my way through the course; it's filled with activities and practical pieces of work to do, all building up to a design that uses the practices and principles learned during the course and from life experiences. I had hoped to complete the course in around six months, but as so often happens in life, other things have presented themselves to fill my time, in particular, writing. I hope to complete the PDC by the end of the year and then take a tutor's course and I look forward to becoming a course tutor to support others who are exploring permaculture.

> Don't let one bad experience stop you from achieving your dreams. Instead, use it as a catalyst for finding another way forward.

PROPAGATING SKILLS

One of the most useful skills I've learnt in the garden is that of propagation. Being able to create more plants from those you already have in the garden (or are given by other gardeners) can save huge amounts of money, especially when propagating a plant that has a higher initial outlay. The other time I've been grateful for this skill is when I want to have a large number of one particular type of plant.

My first experience of propagating from cuttings was in the early 1980s. Geoff Hamilton (on BBC *Gardeners' World*) demonstrated how to take cuttings of a small mauve aster. I didn't quite believe what I was seeing and couldn't fathom that it could be so simple. The next day I spotted some asters being sold at a local fruit and veg shop, so I bought one and took it home to try my hand at growing new plants from cuttings. Within a matter of weeks, the aster cuttings had developed tiny roots and my love of propagating had begun. I found it incredible that a plant could know to grow roots from a cut stem and I started to experiment with cuttings from everything I liked the look of. The basic idea of 'snap a piece off and shove it in the ground' appeals to the lazy gardener in me, while the biological process of a plant creating a different type of cell from the initial tissues fascinates the more enquiring side.

Inevitably, there have been as many failures, if not more so, than successes, but those precious successes spur me on to continue taking cuttings each year. There is something mystical and magical about removing a flowerpot to discover that the dark compost is marbled with creamy white roots. The two plants that I take the most cuttings from are currants of all colours and roses. The currants grow roots readily and have a high success rate, which has allowed me to quickly increase the number of currant bushes in the food forest. Rose cuttings have a much lower rate of success, but those that do grow are celebrated and cherished as each one comes with personal memories attached to it.

An arch that marks the divide between the raised bed vegetable garden and the Patrons' Garden has a red climbing rose scrambling over it. This was grown from a cutting that I took from a plant growing in our previous home; it was hidden behind an evergreen honeysuckle and had grown tall and wispy in its search for light. I don't know the variety, but suspect that it is a Paul's Scarlet as it looks so similar. Regularly, as I wander around the garden, I am reminded of the happy time we spent living in that rented house.

This red rose was grown from a cutting taken at our previous home

One of the advantages of plants grown from cuttings is that they are a clone of the parent plant, so if given the same growing conditions, they will grow in the same way as the plant from which the cutting was taken. This means that it is worth taking the time to choose the specimen to take cuttings from with care, choosing strong healthy plants whenever possible. The exception to this is if I am taking cuttings to try to keep a plant in the garden where the parent plant is potentially dying from old age or if part of a plant is infected with a disease, but there is still unaffected growth. A cutting from the healthy material might allow the continued growth of that variety in the garden.

Propagation by division, layering or by runners also provides a clone of the parent plant and filled me with wonder as I learnt how best to do each method. I was scared that I would kill the plant when I first used division as a means to gain new plants. I could see how lifting a plant from the ground and gently prising it apart or breaking off the outer pieces with some roots attached would create more of the same plant, but the first time I put a spade against a chunky root to chop through it, I winced as I thought about the potential to kill it completely. My fears were unfounded and I was soon merrily chopping up plants to fill the borders of the garden.

Many herbaceous perennials perform better when they have been divided as it prevents overcrowding, giving each section of the plant more space to thrive. Once I knew about this propagation method, I soon saw evidence of it happening naturally. Plants tend to grow outwards, with new shoots appearing from underground on the outside of the older growth and over time the central section can die, leaving the young, vigorous shoots to grow on. Dividing plants mimics their natural growth behaviour, gives me more plants to fill spaces in the garden and is completely free.

I like plants that send out runners; more to the point I like some plants that send out runners. I could happily do without the creeping buttercups that creep their way across any and every part of the garden, unless I am disciplined about removing them on a very regular basis. Strawberries, on the other hand, take all the work out of propagating by sending out a long stem-like growth, a runner, that grows a new plant on the end of it. When the long 'runner' settles on the soil, the new plant will grow and put down roots. All that's needed is to decide whether I'll let it continue to grow in that spot or cut its cord and move it to a new place in the garden. I often see gardeners place a small pot of compost under the new plant and peg it down with a small piece of bent wire and after several months they then detach the new plant and can take the pot with a healthy young plant to a new spot in the garden. This makes sense to me if the young plant is growing against a hard surface like a concrete path or paving slab, but here there are no such pathways. The young plants start growing on the wood chip paths, so I leave them exactly where they grow until I am ready to move them; this saves me money (no pot or compost required), time and energy as I don't need to keep watering them.

Other plants send out runners under the ground, sometimes several feet (metres) away from the parent plant. Raspberries do this with extraordinary vigour and despite having put some of the autumn fruiting raspberries in a raised bed, their runners are popping up in the beds either side. If I wanted more raspberry plants, it would be a relatively simple task to gently lift the new plants and cut them away from the parent plants.

Layering is the method I use least often. Stems or branches are pinned to the ground using a metal pin or a stone and over time they grow roots from a leaf node and also start to develop into a potentially independent plant. Once the roots have grown well, the new plant can be separated from the main plant and moved to a new place in the garden. This happens naturally with plants like honeysuckle, currants and vines and I have found dozens of new honeysuckle plants that have rooted in the wood chips at the front of the house. I have given most of those new fragrant honeysuckles to local residents and a few have been planted in the hedges around the perimeter of the gardens.

I've layered several stems of a grape vine that grows inside the polytunnel; this grapevine was given to us by Tony O'Neill during one of our visits to his allotment. I think that the warmth and shelter inside the tunnel provides an ideal environment for the stems to root quickly, giving us new plants to grow on a little more before I plant them into their permanent positions around the polytunnel. My hope is that in future years these young plants will provide us with plenty of fruit to eat and with which to make wine.

New grape vines propagated by layering

Seed saving is not only a simple way to create more plants, but potentially the number of new plants that can be raised from the seeds of just one plant is huge. I collect seeds whenever I can, to sow the next year.

To have the best chance of growing strong, healthy plants the next year, seeds should be saved from the plants that show the most vigour and the best examples of that particular variety. Seeds saved from weak plants or those displaying uncharacteristic traits may pass on those flaws or weaknesses through their seeds.

Because I know I might want to save seeds for sowing the next year, I tend to grow standard, heirloom or heritage varieties that will grow true to characteristics of the parent plant. While so many plants are offered as F1 varieties with fabulous colours, shapes or sizes, their seeds do not necessarily grow true to the parent plant.

F1 varieties are created by cross-pollinating plant A and plant B to achieve a specific set of genes that display the desired characteristics in plant C. The seeds collected from plant C will not necessarily display the desired traits.

A standard, heritage or heirloom variety will almost always grow true to form, so those seeds are the best to collect and save.

WHEN THINGS ARE OUT OF CONTROL

The warmth of early spring 2019 encouraged masses of blossoms on the fruit trees and we looked set to have a bumper harvest. The huge elderberry tree was so heavily laden with flowers that the softer growth was bending under its weight.

And then May arrived, bringing cooler weather, rain and very blustery winds. Within days the potential harvest of elderberries was blown away as elderflowers littered the ground right across the paddock and yard. The flowers had been destroyed by the winds before the pollinators could get to them and pollinate them. My guess is that in excess of 95% of the blossoms were lost and I made the decision that any fruit that did form would be left on the tree for the wild bird population.

In previous years, I had worked on the basis of 70% for us, 30% for the birds, so I harvested the berries that I could reach fairly easily and used a pole with a hook screwed into the end of it for those a little further out of reach, but I didn't make an attempt to reach the berries highest up, to ensure that the local birds could feast on them. The ripening elderberries beckon the birds and the tree starts to heave with sparrows, starlings, a pair of wood pigeons and collared doves among other species. As they land on the top branches and twigs to

access the berries, the whole tree seems to come alive as it moves and sways under their weight, and their chatter seems to get louder each year.

2019 was not going to be the year of the great elderberry harvest and there would be no new elderberry wine made. As luck would have it, I found a bag of elderberries harvested in 2018 tucked away in the freezer, so they were added to some raspberries and Mr J was able to enjoy raspberry and elderberry wine instead.

I haven't had much luck making elderflower wine; whenever I've tried, it has tasted pretty awful (that's

an understatement), but the elderberries create a wine that is deep, rich and flavoursome. I make very simple, very basic country wines.

When I first made wine, I used a basic recipe from a book that my mother gave to me in the 1970s called *Farmhouse Kitchen* by Audrey Ellis. My country wines are not glamorous, but usually jolly palatable and it didn't take long for Mr J to appreciate the huge savings we made in comparison to buying wine at the supermarket. Previously we had spent around £5–8 per bottle; the homemade wine cost around 25p per bottle.

Juvenile starlings on the elderberry tree

HOW I MAKE A COUNTRY WINE

Ensure all the equipment is clean and sterile.

Extract the flavour from the fruit by either boiling the fruit in water for 10-15 minutes or by pouring boiling water over the fruit and leaving it to stand, covered, for 48 hours.

Put sugar and yeast into a demijohn.

Add the room temperature, fruit-flavoured water, and top it up with water to the base of the neck of the demijohn.

Apply an airlock and leave it to ferment.

Rack the wine after 2-4 weeks and again at approximately three months and six months.

Once fermenting has completely finished, it can be left to mature in the demijohn or be bottled.

Leave in a cool place for 6-18 months.

EATING HABITS

There are other foods and drinks that I make from homegrown produce that also save us a considerable amount of money, but money is not our only motivation. The freshness and quality of the fruit, vegetables, eggs and meat that we can produce, in our opinion, is far higher than anything we can buy in our local shops. During late summer and autumn, I make all the jams, jellies, chutneys and sauces as accompaniments to our meals that we are likely to want in the year ahead. These include strawberry, raspberry and blackcurrant jam, apple and mint, redcurrant, and elderberry jelly. Chutneys include tomato, mixed vegetables, and beetroot with apple. Apple sauce is made in large quantities because it can be used in puddings, as an accompaniment or added to dishes to give them a rich sweetness.

Our meals range from the simplicity of a tray of roasted vegetables to stir-fries and casseroles with complex sauces and they are all cooked on the basis of 'what have we got to eat today?' I rarely plan meals ahead of time as this gives me the flexibility to respond to the warmth (or cold) of the weather, how hungry we are and what else we are doing during the day.

The major change that happened during 2019 is that I no longer make cakes and stodgy puddings on a regular basis. Now desserts are based on fruit, oats and meringue. To help me lose weight, Mr J now has a cupboard of chocolate, biscuits and snacks, made from products that, because of allergies, I cannot eat. It's less tempting to dip into a cupboard full of goodies when you know that they are likely to make you ill. Thoughtfulness like this makes me appreciate him even more.

Mr J is an unfussy eater; there are very few meals that he hasn't enjoyed or if there are, he hasn't told me about them. The freezer is filled with ready meals and pre-prepared side dishes to help ensure that we always have homegrown, homecooked meals to hand.

ANNUAL HABITS

It seems that, despite the successes of the previous years, each spring I go through a phase of being panic-stricken about whether I, or more to the point, the garden can produce enough food for the year ahead.

In the first year, the fear was that we wouldn't be able to create enough raised beds at a time when the ground was so poor, as was my health. The second year it was more of the same, although my health had improved enough to only need a walking stick on occasions when I had overdone things in the previous days.

The third year I felt as though I now had no reason to panic as all the beds were made and I'd been improving the shallow compost and soil in the raised beds, but the inner panic happened all the same. It was not a fleeting thought that flickered through my head, but a deep-seated panic that, over the course of a month or so, pushed its way to the surface and made me grumpy, snappy and, I suspect, rather unpleasant to live with.

The spring of the fourth year was filled with excitement about the new, covered growing space in the polytunnel, but still I hit a wall of doubt and as I write at the start of our fifth growing season, I have once again had a month of feeling panic-stricken and doubting in my abilities and the garden's capacity.

By late May, I start wondering what all the fuss was about as the garden starts to fill with growth and it becomes easy to see the abundance unfolding in front of us. I understand that there are so many factors over which I have no control (like the weather) and, to some extent, I've learnt not to agonise over those things, but I'm still not completely confident that I can achieve even the things that I know I can control, like the planning and processes needed to get the young annual plants into the ground. I feel like there has to be a better way to feed our family than this annual ritual of panic about failing, before the rush to grow annual plants, which eventually leads to an abundance of food and quashes my fears.

PERENNIAL VEGETABLES

I like the idea of perennial vegetables. It seems to me that any plant that comes back year after year and provides a greater harvest each growing season has to be worth exploring. In 2016 I grew some globe artichokes from seed and planted them at the back of the vegetable garden. I had hoped that the silvery foliage would provide a nice backdrop to the veg garden as I looked out at it from the kitchen. What I hadn't factored in was that the trees and shrubs in the food forest would quickly block any view of the vegetables from the house and would provide a colourful, leafy landscape image of their own.

In late 2017 or possibly early 2018, I added asparagus to the vegetable garden. I planted two raised beds with four different varieties of asparagus, hoping that the combination of varieties would provide a long harvesting period.

Asparagus is a long-term commitment; grown from seed it can take four or five years before harvesting, but I bought two-year-old crowns which sped up the process. The first year after planting an asparagus crown it should be left to grow. I'm not sure how many gardeners manage to leave it completely without trying at least one spear. In the second year after planting, a few spears can be harvested and from

> Think of the whole picture, while also looking at the smaller ones and see how one part impacts another.

Asparagus underplanted with lettuce

the third year after planting it should be possible to harvest more and more each year. I think it's worth the wait and, in some ways, those small harvests in the earliest years are all the more special. Freshly harvested asparagus can be eaten raw; the slimmer of the stems have a sweetness that seems lost in the cooking process and seems altogether absent in the vegetable when purchased in shops and supermarkets. I cook asparagus lightly in boiling water (unsalted) and serve it with a little melted butter, sea salt and coarse ground black pepper. We also like it topped with a poached egg to dip the spears into. It's messy food and more often than not, we end up with either butter or egg yolk on our chins.

With an increased interest in growing perennial vegetables, I searched online for vegetables to grow so that we could test the taste of them. I was pleasantly surprised at the number of perennial vegetables that will grow in the UK and wondered why they are not more commonly grown.

Perhaps it is a result of nurturing – if our parents, guardians or significant others didn't grow them, then we are unlikely to have been exposed to them, so we don't know about them and continue growing the same foods that we are familiar with.

Or perhaps it is a result of commercial forces; after all, there's less profit to be made from selling seeds once than there is from selling new seeds every year. And it could be that as industrial, monoculture farming increased and seeds were selected not for their taste, but for uniformity, volume and ease of harvest, we forgot about the alternatives to the narrow range of veg on offer to us on the shelves of most shops.

As gardeners at home, we have the potential to rediscover some of the huge range of vegetables with their myriad of tastes. The perennial vegetables include:

asparagus	Taunton Deane kale
globe artichoke	rhubarb
Jerusalem artichoke	skirret
Chinese artichoke	sweet cicely
Caucasian spinach	walking onions
cardoon	walking stick cabbage
Good King Henry	perennial leeks
oca	horseradish
nine star broccoli	sea kale
Daubenton kale	Welsh onions (bunching)

There is also a host of plants that are usually grown in the ornamental garden that have edible parts, not just the flowers (which I've added to salads for colour and interest), but also stems, roots and leaves. The handful that I grow include hosta, Solomon's seal, some varieties of daylilies and roses.

Have we been missing out on a great swathe of tastes and textures that we could have been enjoying in our meals? I don't know because I still haven't tried many of them. As much as I'd like to think we are becoming more adventurous in our eating habits, the reality is that we generally stick to the same few familiar vegetables that we know and love. We are slowly increasing the number of varieties within each veg group, but we haven't chosen to dive in head first and try all the edibles available to us.

GROWING UNDER COVER

Growing in a polytunnel was a new experience for me and I was delighted at the ease with which I could now grow a useful number of warmth-loving plants.

Once we had put the cover on the frame and constructed the doors, I needed to decide whether to grow in raised beds or directly into the ground. I chose the latter as I thought it might give slugs and snails fewer places to hide and offer more potential for the layout of beds.

I put weed suppressing membrane on each side of the tunnel and created a central path by putting chopped rapeseed straw on the ground.

I was so enamoured with the polytunnel that I thought about putting a camp bed in it and moving in. It may have only been a passing thought, but as I merrily sowed seeds and planted seedlings, it passed through my mind on more than one occasion.

Within a couple of months, I had pulled back the membrane on one side to create a full-length bed and I planted tomatoes through the membrane on the other side. This gave me four distinct areas in which to grow, but the soil was not friable; it was still the heavy clay of the paddock. I laid empty chicken feed sacks onto the grassy ground and put compost on it to give a good start to the seeds I wanted to sow and young seedlings that I had ready to plant.

It was mid-April by the time I started planting in the polytunnel so I didn't experience the possibilities for extending the growing season at the start of the year, but I did plant melons, which I'd never grown before, and looked forward to growing the heat-loving plants. The cucumber and tomato harvests were plentiful as was the supply of salad leaves and mustard greens. I grew an aubergine (eggplant) for the first time and despite disliking the large deep purple aubergines that I've previously bought in shops, these small finger-like aubergines were almost sweet and we were both surprised at enjoying them so much.

When I harvested the first melon, I was so excited. I hot-footed it inside, clasping my precious fruit to my chest so that I didn't drop and damage it (think Gollum at high speed). When I cut into it, the aroma was almost cloyingly sweet and as I scooped out the seeds, the cavity left by them filled with melon juice. I'd like to say that I politely cut it into neat slices, but I didn't. I quartered it and ate it straight from the skin, juices running down my chin and dripping onto the kitchen work surface. It was the sweetest tasting, best melon I've ever eaten and can only describe it as ambrosia.

Then I hit a dilemma; Mr J wasn't home from work yet and the other half of the melon beckoned. I think if I hadn't been so proud of having been able to grow such a splendid fruit, I would have eaten the second half and not said anything about it, but as it was, I wanted to share with him just how fabulous a thing I had grown. The other melons harvested that summer were, in theory, just as lovely, but none of them were as sweet as the first.

In early autumn I planted pea seeds in guttering in which I had previously drilled some drainage holes. I suspended the guttering in the tunnel using baler twine and for weeks during the cold, dark, late autumn and early winter, we had fresh pea shoots to add to our meals. I sowed beetroot seeds for them to overwinter in the polytunnel for an early beetroot harvest and winter lettuces provided fresh salad leaves right through until spring.

I feel as though I still haven't got to grips with the potential of growing under cover in a polytunnel, so the experiments of timings and possibilities continue.

THE START OF PERMANENCE IN THE GARDEN

Despite the transient nature of most of the structures, the polytunnel, archways, raised beds, perennial plants and trees have given the garden a sense of solid permanence. The perennial vegetables and trees provide a living framework around which the annual planting performs its fleeting dance before dying away at the end of the year.

The arched tunnel between the Patrons' Garden and the market garden area has two climbing roses growing up it and, I hope, in time they will completely cover the tunnel-shading out light for weeds to grow in the pathway, while also filling the air with their heady perfume.

The fruit, nut and other trees are no longer spindly whips and are casting dappled shade on the ground around them, adding height and form and a sense of maturity to the landscape.

The speckled white trunks of four silver birch trees add some drama and although I planted them as purely ornamental trees, I have since learnt that the sap can be extracted and used to make a drink, although as yet I'm not rushing out to tap the trees for their sap.

Looking at these more permanent features, I realise that at some point during this year there was a shift in emphasis, from creating a new garden to tending a maturing one. With this change came a confidence, of knowing how the garden responds to the elements and, apart from my annual blip in faith, that this space could produce more food than could be consumed by just the two of us.

A MICRO CSA

After nearly a year of research and reading, I decided that this was the year that I would take the plunge and launch a Community Supported Agriculture (CSA) veg box scheme. The idea behind it is that local residents agree to buy a veg box per week for X numbers of weeks. By knowing at the start of the growing season how much food would need to be grown to fill the vegetable boxes, it is easier to plan the growing season.

Here's the information that I now have about our CSA veg boxes on the Byther Farm website.

BYTHER FARM

It's not just a veg box scheme!

Community Supported Agriculture (CSA) benefits both customers (members) and food producers (farmers).

When you agree to become a member of Byther Farm CSA, you will be able to build a closer relationship to the food you are eating, you'll be able to visit the farm, talk with us and see how we grow. You'll be supporting the local economy and ensuring that your food hasn't travelled the earth to reach your table. And it helps us as farmers to use ecological methods which benefit our environment whilst still being highly productive.

As a member of Byther Farm CSA you'll be committing to paying for a whole season's worth of vegetables as the season begins. This will help us to accurately plan and budget for the seeds and materials that we will need for the year ahead.

Using a CSA, the farmer and the consumer can share in the risks and rewards that come with producing food locally, seasonally and naturally. In a nutshell, this means accepting that the success of each and every crop varies from year to year, which means sharing the low yields as well as the highs of an abundant harvest.

By purchasing a 'share' of the vegetables and fruit that we produce you will become an active and valued member of our small farm. You will also be invited to visit the farm to see how and where your food is grown.

Other benefits of a CSA 'share' membership:

Customers

Direct selling allows for a fairer price for both us and you.

Fresh produce, picked on the day of delivery and fewer miles travelled.

Our crops are grown without the use of artificial pesticides, herbicides and other chemically based products.

You will be eating seasonally which means your food should contain higher levels of essential micronutrients (with all the benefits that can come with this).

Farmers

Growing vegetables and fruit requires a large amount of careful planning and organising months before the first crop is harvested and by knowing we have the commitment from members at this time provides us with invaluable support.

By knowing the volumes of vegetables and fruit which we will need to grow, we can reduce wastage by only growing what is needed.

Knowing where the food we produce is going and who it will be feeding makes us feel even more keen to grow and proud to be farmers.

FINDING CUSTOMERS, BUILDING A MEMBERSHIP

It's all very well having the belief that enough food can be grown to be able to sell it, but none of that matters without a customer base to become members of the scheme. I've found that the most effective way to reach potential customers is to use pre-established networks. Having created the information page on my website, I put a post on a local community group on Facebook asking if anyone might be interested in a locally grown veg box and I waited for a response. Just as had happened when I asked about eggs, the responses came flooding in and for days I spent my evenings replying to queries and explaining how the scheme would work.

After about a week, seven potential members had agreed to take a veg box each week for the season, which I decided would last for 20 weeks. This felt like a manageable size for the first year, especially as I hadn't planned for it right at the start of the growing season, so the bulk of the veg box contents would have to come from plants that I'd already grown and anything that I could grow during the summer months.

We talked about the best containers for delivery until we had gone round in circles. We wanted to use something that was strong enough to take the weight of the veg and something that could be washed regularly. I looked at jute bags, recycled fabric bags, cardboard boxes and a host of other potential containers. I decided to buy secondhand plastic stacking crates, much like those used by supermarkets for home deliveries of foods. I sourced some half size crates which looked perfect for the job. They can be stacked away neatly when not in use and could be washed thoroughly each week. I bought 20 so that one could be with the veg box scheme members during the week and a second would be here and ready to be filled. Then all we needed to do was deliver the veg in one crate and collect the empty crate from the previous week. This worked perfectly; the plastic is being used over and over again and during the winter months I could use them for storing squashes, onions, hand tools and anything else that needed to be kept tidily in one place.

I requested that members pay for their veg boxes two weeks in advance and most paid monthly in advance, but in hindsight I should have pushed gently for them to pay for the whole season at the start as I spent quite a lot of time chasing payments or checking that payments had been made.

> Building a good relationship with each CSA member is worth every second of your time. They may want to get to know you, your growing space and working practices before committing to a veg box.

It took a little while for members to get to grips with the volume of food that was delivered in their boxes. The start of the season gave smaller amounts of just a few vegetables. I aimed to put at least seven different types of vegetables in each box, including lettuce and salad leaves and some herbs. By late July and early August, the boxes were overflowing with courgettes (zucchini), cucumbers and beans; later in the year there was an abundance of kale and cabbages. One member asked whether they could change to having a box on alternate weeks as they couldn't eat it all in one week; I realised that I hadn't explained adequately that they would need to process or share, with friends and family, the contents of the box as more and more produce was included.

I decided that the next year I would stress to potential members that they would need to be prepared to process, freeze, dry or give away the surplus in their boxes. I also told myself that it would be worth spending a little time at the start of the year finding members who were prepared to pay for the whole year in advance as it would save so much mental energy over the year if I didn't need to be chasing payments or checking that payments had arrived in the bank account. When I opened the booking system for membership for the 2020 season, it was sold out of the 20 memberships on offer in less than 24 hours and I was pleased to see so many members from the first year return: a sure sign that we were doing something right. I requested payment in advance in one, two or four payments, all of which were made before deliveries started and I found it much easier to manage. I also decided to list and show an image of each veg box's contents on the website together with a few suggestions for use.

Some vegetables are great for using in the veg boxes and others I grow just for our own use. Globe artichokes make an impressive display in a veg box, but the plants need plenty of room to

Globe artichokes

grow, and produce their flower buds for a relatively short period; as a perennial they then sit in the ground taking up potential growing space for other, quicker to mature, crops.

The staple veg for the boxes are onions, carrots, garlic, beetroots, salads and legumes. I chose varieties that I'm familiar with and I know crop consistently well in our garden; it was a distinct advantage to know what usually grows well here. The other vegetables that fill the boxes were either faster growing foods like spring onions (scallions), mustard leaves, rocket, radishes, turnips or more seasonal vegetables like brassicas (spring cabbage, summer cabbage, red cabbage, kales, kalettes, Brussels sprouts, swedes/rutabaga) and later in the year tomatoes and squashes. When we had a glut of fruit, I included those in the boxes too.

> The food grown for veg boxes isn't always the same as food grown for home consumption. Don't get so focussed on growing for others that you forget to grow the varieties of food that you like to eat.

GSOH ESSENTIAL

Life isn't all seriousness all the time and I feel that the garden should reflect this. I know that some people like garden ornaments and painted gnomes to add humour to their gardens. I decided to have a scarecrow. I was prompted by a content creator on YouTube, who invited me to take part in a video collaboration about making a scarecrow. I knew I didn't want to have a traditional style scarecrow made from clothes stuffed with straw, and in any case, that wouldn't stand up to the winds and rain for very long, so I looked around for a suitable alternative.

In the barn I had a metal dressmaker's dummy style ornament. A heavy-duty wire framework that looked like a dress. It had a matching stand and was designed to be a piece of home decoration.

I have always liked the idea of having some topiary in the garden, the clipped foliage making the desired shape. I wondered whether I could combine the scarecrow and topiary and grow a plant up and through the wire framework.

I pushed a long piece of hazel pole through the 'armholes' and attached the grandchildren's out-grown mittens to each end and then hung a pair of children's wellington boots from the skirt of the dress to form legs and feet. A rather ornate sunhat, that had been bought years before for a wedding I'd attended and now had bird poop on it, became the scarecrow's head.

It may not be the most effective of scarecrows, but it was fun to make and brings a smile when I see it in the garden nestled among the branches of the elderberry tree in the centre of the Patron's Garden.

I still haven't found the right plant to grow through the framework to create the topiary scare-crow, but no doubt I will find just the right one in time. And because no respecting scarecrow should be without a name, I called her Doris.

Doris, the scarecrow

HEALTH AND WELFARE

Although the weather wasn't as hot or sunny as the previous year, this felt like a good year. The garden was developing into a more mature space with interesting corners and vistas, I was growing plenty of food for our family and for others, and I was finally losing some of the weight that I had been carrying around with me.

Hand in hand with the loss of excess weight, I also lost some excess baggage: a sadness and emotional heaviness that had been lurking in the background unacknowledged, but weighing me down emotionally. It seems that as the garden has developed, so have I.

It has taken our time here for me to learn to fully work with the seasons, to give myself permission to rest and recuperate during the darker, colder months and to listen to my body's need to stop and be still. Also, to accept that I sleep very little during the height of summer and although I am starting to get tired, there is more work to do in the early autumn than any other time of year. This annual rhythm suits me and the more I have allowed myself to listen to and respond to the seasons, the better I have felt, physically and emotionally.

My confidence also grew: confidence in the garden's capacity, in my ability to nurture plants to maturity and in my ability to share, via videos, our journey to abundance and self-sufficiency.

By the end of autumn, I had lost around 45 pounds (20 kilos) and was buying clothes three or four sizes smaller than at the start of the year. My knees, hips, feet and back ached less and my skin looked healthier. The negative inner voice, that I allow to creep into my thoughts when I'm low, nagged me that I should have lost the weight sooner, but I also know that there is no point in trying to lose weight or stop any unhealthy habit until I'm in the right headspace. I was so glad that I decided that this was the year to address the excess weight, because I was going to start the new decade feeling healthier and happier than I had for almost the whole of the previous ten years.

Feeling positive about the future, I decided that in the coming 12 months I would run several more workshops and courses at Byther Farm. Starting in November 2019, I ran a series of workshops creating Christmas wreaths from scratch using materials from the garden.

Enough participants wanted to make a natural wreath that I could run a workshop each weekend for a month. It reminded me just how much I like running workshops and courses and encouraged by the response, I designed a Soft Fruit Gardening workshop for the next spring. These also proved popular despite being held in the lead-up to storms Ciara and Dennis and not being able to spend much time outside because of the rising wind speeds and rain. By the end of March, travel restrictions and social distancing regulations introduced in response to the COVID-19 pandemic put a stop to further courses later in the spring and summer. Not wanting to be held back by this, I decided to develop an online course, which will be released as soon as it's completed.

Although winter is still a difficult time, I have learnt to celebrate even the smallest of successes and take joy in all tasks achieved. The constant positive messages I give myself have, no doubt, played a major role in the continued improvement I feel both physically and mentally, as has the healthier range of food that we now enjoy.

Workshop participants, Libby and Charlotte, with their wreaths

MAXIMISING THE USE OF GROWING SPACE

One of the key elements to ensuring that we have a constant supply of fresh vegetables to harvest, as well as enough stored away for the winter months, is successional sowing and planting. We have a rolling programme of sowing a few seeds at a time, to ensure that crops mature and are ready to harvest at a staggered rate throughout the growing seasons. It has taken a while to get used to the microclimate here and to get a feel for how long each fruit or vegetable will need to reach maturity and be ready to harvest. I still get the timings wrong on a regular basis, but there is usually enough food of a similar taste or use to see us through until the next harvest is ready in a few weeks' time.

I also try to make sure that I have young plants ready to fill any spaces made from harvesting a crop. In reality this often means that I have plants that are bordering on pot bound and, if they don't get planted, will end up on the compost heap. I've decided that I would rather it be this way round than find that I have void spaces in the raised beds.

Another useful method is to interplant crops. As one vegetable starts to grow and mature, I plant a different type of vegetable in between the first plants. This works particularly well with quick growing vegetables like radish and mustards when sown between taller plants like brassicas e.g. kale and Brussels sprouts. I've also planted corn and squash between onions so they have a chance to establish themselves before I harvest the onions and that worked well too. The stacking of layers of vegetables in the beds can allow for growing twice or three times as much food from the same amount of space.

The hungry gap can be a tricky time of year. During April, May and June most of the vegetables that have grown during the winter are coming to an end, but the spring and summer harvests are not yet ready. Over the last few years, I've been experimenting with different ways to eke out the winter veg a little longer and now we have the polytunnel I can grow earlier in the season to give us a wider variety of fresh food all year round. I have chosen some varieties of leeks, cabbages, purple sprouting broccoli and Brussels sprouts that are late to mature and by sowing them in two or three batches about three weeks apart, I have been able to spread out the harvesting period a little longer. I've chosen varieties of spring vegetables that are ready to harvest very early in the season like rhubarb Timperley Early, which has been ready to harvest from mid to late March, right through to late July. And the garlic bulbs that I forgot to lift and harvest in the previous

> Sow or plant little and often whenever you can, so there is a constant supply of vegetables ready to harvest fresh. This saves there being a glut of vegetables that need to be processed and stored.

year produced green shoots that I could cut and use in the kitchen and shortly afterwards, their young bulbs.

I planted some winter lettuces in the polytunnel and some more from the same sowing in the garden, to see what the difference would be to their growth. Those in the garden limped through winter, despite it being very mild, if rather wet. During the first flush of warm weather in very early spring, they suddenly bolted and started to run to seed. The lettuce in the polytunnel grew evenly and well and offered us plenty of salad leaves right through April and May. In future years I will plant a similar number in the polytunnel in late autumn to provide us with winter salads.

YEAR END EVALUATION AND PLANS

As the end of the year drew near, our annual evaluation of the year was filled with 'that worked well' or 'that was better than expected' and other positive statements. We also talked about the potential impact of political and social events across the world.

Since 2016, I have been slowly putting away a few items of food and household products that will store well, so that we have a few emergency stores, should we need them. We agreed to continue this practice for the foreseeable future, just a few extra items in the shopping basket every now and then to gently stockpile the non-perishable goods that we buy in.

We decided to expand the veg box scheme and have more members and I suggested that I try to preserve even more food in the year ahead, so that if there were food shortages, like those being predicted, we would have saved resources to rely on. We discussed that I continue to be concerned that there may be medication shortages and that, because of the way that our local surgery issues prescriptions, I only ever have a maximum of 28 days' tablets at any one time. I worry about the impact that being without the thyroid medicines might have.

With Mr J, discussing our plans for the next year

We agreed to reduce the chicken flock still further and not to keep chickens for a while. This would allow me to concentrate on building the duck flock. We also chose not to keep any turkeys in the year ahead and to use all the available space in the food forest for growing fruit and vegetables.

COVID-19 was starting to make the news from China and while we were aware and a little concerned about what that might mean in the future, we had no idea how great an impact it was about to have.

HARVESTING AND STORING – CANNING/BOTTLING

Canning or bottling is the process of preserving foods using high temperatures and in a domestic setting, it's usually done in glass jars. There are two types of canning, water bath and pressure canning. I have done some basic water bath canning in the past for high-acid foods like apple sauce. The next step would be to learn how to pressure can.

I watched several 'how to' videos and decided that it really can't be too difficult to do; all I needed

was to buy a pressure canner, which is different to a pressure cooker and, with the support of a good canning book, to gain the confidence to use it. Buying a pressure canner in the UK is not as easy as I had hoped and I looked at how cost effective it would be to import one from the USA. Eventually a friend of a friend sent one from America. It sat in my kitchen for months, unused, reminding me of my inadequacies in food preservation skills.

carrots   parsnips
root parsley   celery   celeriac
beet leaves   chard   leeks
Brussels sprouts
kale   kalettes
purple sprouting broccoli
Taunton Deane kale
parsley   chives
garlic (grown as a perennial)
lettuce   Asturian tree cabbage
raspberries   potatoes
cabbage   runner beans
borlotti beans   dill   fennel
marjoram   thyme
bay   rosemary   squashes
apples   pears   calendula
Greek gigantes beans
sweetcorn   yacon
oca   pea shoots
tomatoes   melon

YEAR FIVE

2020

CONSTANT CHANGES

Ways I'm Wealthy Without Money

There are moments in most days and sometimes whole days when I feel very wealthy. I have almost no money, no savings, no little nest egg, no rainy day fund and yet I feel rich. How can that be? Well, I am rich with things that matter to me and as long as I have just about enough money to pay for the things I have to pay for, it's these other things that are more important.

Family

The love of my family gives me a feeling of belonging and of security. Although I don't see my brothers very often (as they live on the other side of the Atlantic), there is a constant and a grounding feeling of knowing that they are there, unseen and often unspoken to, but there all the same. My sister would be a close friend if she was not my sister; we share the same values, sense of duty, honour and compassion and we have a similar sense of humour and laugh hard at the same things which often leaves us in tears and with aching sides. My daughter is a mini-me (she probably won't thank me for saying so!), although she is brighter, has more sparkle and is heaps wiser than I was at her age. I love her unconditionally and by the bucket-load. My two grandsons are a surprising source of love; I had heard all the sayings about grandchildren being even better than having children and not really understood what was meant, and now I do! Those two little boys evoke a gush of love every time I think about them; I can see their good and less endearing traits (and we all have those!) and love them anyway.

Friends

I have a small group of friends that have been part of my life for a very long time. We don't always see each other regularly, but we do communicate one way or another on a semi-regular basis. We've been through good times together and been there when the bad times have gripped us, celebrated our personal happiness and supported each other through sad times. More recent friends also bring delight and sparkle, these friendships built on shared interests and laughter.

Love and Laughter

These are two things that I don't want to be without. As long as I feel love for others, feel loved and can find things to laugh about, I know that I am doing alright. Finding love after 50 with Mr J has been the most wonderful experience. Between us we have a little wisdom that comes with learning from the errors of previous relationships. Rather than tiptoe-ing around what could be sensitive subjects (like money, our values, our expectations) we had open and frank discussions when we decided to move in together, finding a way that we could build a solid basis for our relationship and so far it works, it works really well. I find laughter a great healer and binder; it lifts my spirits for much longer than the time it takes to laugh, it has a lasting and lingering impact and makes me feel closer to those I laugh with.

Good Food and Health

Nowadays I know that my health is inextricably linked to what I'm eating and drinking, not just on a general level but on a minute, intricate level. I've had to change what I eat, when I eat and how I eat. We are working towards producing enough of our own food so that we will only need to purchase a few items and for those we will try to source local organically produced foods. There are some obvious exceptions, for example, I don't think there are many locally grown bananas in our corner of south

east Wales. So I have come to appreciate the benefits of good food and value my health and well-being.

Space to Think

This doesn't need to be physical space, but it does need to be the time and a place with relative quiet. When I worked in a very busy office with a small call centre at one side and marketing department on the other and my desk slap-bang between the two, I could hardly hear myself think, so I used to go into work earlier than anyone else and have an hour or so on my own to gather my thoughts for the day, write plans and proposals and anything else that wasn't just responsive or reactive to the hectic office during normal working hours. I used to leave an hour earlier than my co-workers too, which I am not sure went down too well and I used my drive home (which took the best part of an hour) to think. Now I have both the time and physical space to think. As an early riser, I use the first hour or so of the day to think about anything I want to mull over and I have fabulous views to look at while I am thinking.

Fresh Air

When I am outside, in the garden, at a rugby match or in the countryside, I enjoy the cold air on my face or the warmth of the sun on my skin. Our new home has fresh air by the bucket-load. The breeze that constantly comes from the estuary can sometimes be overwhelming, but mostly it brings with it a steady flow of fresh, clean air that I find uplifting and refreshing. Working in the garden gives me ample chance to be out in the fresh air and even on days when it's pouring with rain and blowing a hooley, I need to go out to feed and care for the animals. I like those blasts of cold; they blow away the cobwebs, help to clear my mind and make me all the more appreciative of the cosy warmth of our home when I come back inside.

So there it is, wealth without money. There are lots of other things that make me feel rich and I make sure that I not only notice them, but also appreciate them regularly; after all, there's little point in being so wealthy without enjoying it.

Excerpt from 25th March 2016 – as applicable today as it was back then.

The year started with a trip away. I went to the Oxford Real Farming Conference; it was the first time for half a decade that Mr J and I had been apart for so long. Five years earlier it would have been unimaginable that I would travel independently and spend two days walking around Oxford, meeting people, joining in discussions from nine in the morning until early evening and beyond. I was exhausted, but it was worth every moment. I was surrounded by people who have a similar approach to me to working with the land and I came home inspired, excited and looking forward to the year ahead.

The spring storms wreaked havoc on the oldest of the fruit trees. Storm Ciara left the tallest of the plum trees at a jaunty angle and Storm Dennis ripped across the site taking the plum tree with it, so it is now anchored to the earth by just one small section of root. We decided to leave it in its horizontal position to see whether it might still give us one last harvest before we took it out of the ground. For the first time since we moved here, we have been able to reach the plums and as if the tree knows it is near the end, it has fruited abundantly and given us masses of sweet, juicy plums.

I went through my annual panic about my ability and the garden's capacity to produce enough food and whether there would be enough members to run the CSA veg box scheme. I had no need to worry at all; the harvests have been plentiful and the veg boxes sold out in less than 24 hours after I advertised them. No sooner had the members signed up for the veg boxes, and I mean the next day, movement restrictions were announced in response to the increasing spread of COVID-19. Food shortages were predicted and loo roll disappeared from the supermarket shelves. Alongside retail staff, postal workers, cleaners and of course, nurses and doctors, food growers were suddenly once again being appreciated as the key workers we really are.

Mr J continued in his role as a postal worker, and due to colleagues needing to shield or self-isolate

coupled with the huge increase in people using mail order for everything from paperclips to televisions and patio furniture, he was busier than ever. He went to the local supermarket and ran all the errands and I remained on site for 19 weeks. I needed little excuse to stay at home and grow food; it gave me a good reason to get the market garden completed and produce as much food as I could.

I was delighted to see so many of the flowers that I planted in the Patrons' Garden last year had made it through the winter and were flourishing in the mild spring and summer. The undisturbed days gave me even more space to think and reflect, to soak up the atmosphere in the garden and to notice that, in response to the quiet and stillness of the world outside, the wildlife moved in by the droves. There was a noticeable increase in the numbers of small wildlife and wild birds now making our food forest their home. Dozens of sparrows, a second pair of collared doves, finches with flashes of colour as they fly, noisy blackbirds, friendly robins and yet more wrens whizz and circle around me as I potter around the garden.

The lockdown reminded me of those first few months here, when I didn't feel up to going anywhere, except this year there were no walking sticks, no struggling to stay awake or twitchy, jerking limbs and no new garden to build. This year the winds didn't blow all the blossoms from the trees and there was a bumper harvest of cherries and elderberries. I had plenty of time to sow seeds, weed raised beds and create new structures. The vegetable gardens and food forest provided an abundance of food, not only for our family but for 20 others through the veg box scheme.

I didn't leave our smallholding from mid-March until mid-July, when Mr J and I headed to a nearby town to do administrative paperwork. Four weeks later, we returned to the same offices to exchange some vows.

AFTERWORD BY MR J

It's certainly been a busy few years – especially for Liz. Reading through her book and looking through the photographs showing the development of Byther Farm over the past four years, I've been reminded and, frequently, astounded by how much has been achieved. I probably don't tell Liz often enough just how proud I am of her and of what she's creating, and maybe I do grumble (a little) when I'm asked to help with something heavy or awkward just as the wind is at its peak or the rain is slicing across the plot like a scythe.

I know that neither of us really anticipated that we'd be where we are now when we first moved in and started work on the plot. I really do love that everything has evolved.

There have been constant changes as the space has shown what is best for it and as Liz's (and to an extent my) knowledge of how to maximise the usefulness of our plot without causing any damage, even better while improving its quality, has increased. The days of wormless soil are – thankfully – well behind us, as our local mole population know to their benefit.

It's been good, too, to (re)discover long dormant skills of my own. Building some of the structures around the chicken run; the original raised beds; the bean support structure which is designed to withstand the windiest of weather (though I hope it never gets put to the test in hurricane force winds), together with a host of other building, patching and creating projects have shown me that I too can do it if I put my mind to it. I am happy to have played a supporting role for Liz in the physical side of our work here, as much as I hope I do in the emotional and mental aspects of running our smallholding.

Actually, that's another aspect of growth and change which we don't always notice, because of course we're in the middle of it, but which this book has definitely highlighted for me. Liz's physical and mental health have improved hugely since we moved in. I too can say that I honestly feel the benefits of the work here – as well as the physical aspects of my paid work off-site – on my mental and physical self. I feel calmer than I have done in years. The reduction in day-to-day pressures – or perhaps I should say the change in day-to-day pressures, because we have plenty of them although they are very different to those encountered when working in a nine to five environment

– coupled with the noted health benefits of fresh air, exercise and good quality, organic, locally sourced food (we talk about food feet rather than food miles here) are something I didn't know would have such a massively positive impact on my life. Now they are something I would never move away from.

We've had a lot of discussions, made lots of plans – some of which have come to fruition, some of which haven't and more which have changed even as we started carrying them out – and we have laughed an awful lot together as we (by which I mean mainly Liz) have conducted our stewardship of this space over the past few years. I hope we haven't let it down. I think we've been good to it and, judging by the rewards it has given us, I'd say we have.

Has it been easy? No, it's been hard work and there have been moments where either one of us – fortunately not simultaneously – have wondered why on earth we're doing this, but these pass and talking always helps. I'm really glad we're here, that we've evolved what was a blank and bland field into a bountiful plot of sustenance and, goodness me, I'm looking forward to what comes next.

REFERENCES, RESOURCES & GRATITUDE

BYTHER FARM

Our website can be found at bytherfarm.com
Follow our continuing journey via the YouTube channel Liz Zorab –
    Byther Farm youtube.com/LizZorab
Or on other social media:
    Patreon patreon.com/LizZorab
    Facebook page BytherFarm
    Instagram Liz_Zorab_Byther_Farm
Byther Farm is not currently open to the public.

GRATITUDE

Thanks to Maddy and Tim Harland for convincing me to record this journey, for the guidance and support, and for believing in my ability to write this book, even (and especially) when I faltered.

Thanks to all of the team at Permanent Publications for their patience and enthusiasm.

To Huw Richards, thank you for being my sounding board, and for your friendship and kindness.

To Jane, thank you for your constant friendship, gardening wisdom and willingness to work so hard in the garden whenever you visit us.

Thanks to my sister, Julia, for continuing to inspire me to reach for everything I believe in.

With special thanks to Cecily, for the love, faith and for being wise beyond your years.

And my love, thanks and gratitude to Mr J for your patience, encouragement and unerring support throughout this process (and for the endless cups of tea).

Mr J and I would also like to thank the community of viewers of our YouTube channel and all of our supporters on Patreon.

IMAGES

With the exception of a couple of photographs which were taken by Huw Richards and the cover photo (Jason Ingram), all of the images in this book were taken by myself or Mr J, who lovingly captured our first couple of years here in photographs and unlike me (who tends to hit the delete button on an all too regular basis), he carefully saved them for posterity.

YOUTUBE CHANNELS THAT INSPIRE ME

Gold Shaw Farm
Happen Films
Huw Richards
James Prigioni
Permaculture Magazine
Richard Perkins
Tap O' Noth Farm
The Weedy Garden

WEBSITES

Permaculture Magazine
permaculture.co.uk

Permaculture Women's Guild
permaculturewomen.com

CSA Network UK
communitysupportedagriculture.org.uk

Ridgedale Permaculture
ridgedalepermaculture.com

Freecycle Network UK
freecycle.org

Kafkadiva
kafkadiva.com

And one final thanks –
To all the women across the world who, in the face of adversity, run small farms and grow food, you are my heroines.

INDEX

Enjoyed this book?
You might also like these
from Permanent Publications

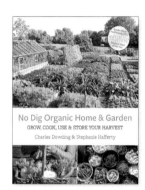

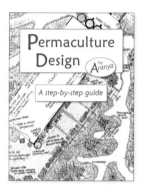

Edible Paradise
Vera Greutink
£16.00
Create your own no dig
garden using permacul-
ture techniques. Grow a
feast for the eyes and the
dinner tables with herbs,
vegetables and flowers.

**Forest Gardening
in Practice**
Tomas Remiarz
£24.95
Step-by-step instructions
for creating your own
forest garden with 14
real-life examples from
Europe and the USA.

**No Dig Organic
Home & Garden**
Charles Dowing
& Stephanie Hafferty
£23.00
Learn how to create your
own no dig vegetable
garden and then preserve
and cook your harvests.

Permaculture Design
Aranya
£15.95
A useful guide for
learning how to use
permaculture design
methods. Based on years
of Aranya's courses with
student feedback.

Our titles cover:

permaculture, home and garden, green building,
food and drink, sustainable technology,
woodlands, community, wellbeing and so much more

Available from all good bookshops and online
retailers, including the publisher's online shop:

https://shop.permaculture.co.uk

with 10% off the RRP on all books

Our books are also available via our American distributor, Chelsea Green:
www.chelseagreen.com/publisher/permanent-publications

Permanent Publications also publishes *Permaculture Magazine*

Enjoyed this book?
Why not subscribe
to our magazine

Available as print and digital subscriptions, all with
FREE digital access to our complete 29 years
of back issues, plus bonus content

Each issue of *Permaculture Magazine* is hand crafted,
sharing practical, innovative solutions, money saving
ideas and global perspectives from a grassroots
movement in over 150 countries

To subscribe visit:

www.permaculture.co.uk

or call 01730 776 582 (+44 1730 776 582)